by Neville

ANATOMY OF A SOCIETY

IN LETTERS

A simple man's search for the truth about life, love and the hereafter

Anatomy of a Society

by Neville Lewis

Preamble

After experiencing substantial difficulties in his job with a small firm, in desperation the author, at the age of 57, began saying this simple prayer: "Dear Lord, please take care of my will and my life this day, because I cannot manage on my own!" The events which followed and the letters he was inspired to write are described in the pages which follow, while every effort has been made, because I respect them all, to conceal the identities of all who were closely involved in my story.

Anatomy of a Society

by Neville Lewis

My Step 4

To the 'Survivors' Magazine

One day when I am well I hope I'll see the truth as it was, the cause of all my pain, and the way it could or should have been in a better more enlightened world.

The crazy hopes and dreams of an angry, frightened little boy in conflict with the world and himself had finally reached their conclusion of despair and disillusion at the age of twenty-one in an agonising onslaught of anxiety and depression.

Drugs were given which helped me through the worst of the trauma and my depression gradually lifted. I had survived the most horrendous experience of my life with my reason spared but my confidence battered and broken.

How I wish I had then had sufficient counselling or psychotherapy to lift me over the final hurdle and kick the tablet habit which now seemed so necessary for my continuing recovery. Perhaps if I had realised then that no tablet could ever cure my emotional problems and enable me to come to terms with myself and the real world around me; perhaps if I had then had the help I needed I might have emerged successfully into adulthood untrammelled by the self-effacing timidity which has hung like a chain around me for most of my life.

But it was not to be. My vision was blurred by the beguiling conviction that tablets would somehow restore my shattered confidence, just as they had relieved the worst symptoms of my depression. Indeed, did my doctors not continue obligingly to dispense my anti-depressants and tranquillisers month by month, year upon year as though they too believed in their curative power?

I now believe the opposite to be true, that the tablets merely prolonged my suffering by allowing the disordered feelings they suppressed to lie dormant within, still active enough to disturb my peace of mind and undermine my ability to function successfully.

Moreover the tablets brought their own measure of gratuitous misery in the form of vicious, subtle side-effects such as poor concentration, disturbing feelings of agitation, bouts of acute tiredness and, perhaps worst of all, a dampening effect on the more pleasurable feelings such as those moments of sheer poetry which help to sustain us through life's difficulties, the sense of awe and rapture one can feel at the beauty of a splendid sunset, the incredible symmetry of a snowflake or the magnificent sound of a well-loved symphony. Such feelings seem to have been missing or tenuous at best for many years without my knowing, yet now I am feeling them again with renewed awareness and eagerness - now that I am once again coming off my tranquillisers!

by Neville Lewis

36 years have passed since my breakdown, and again, despite many painful failed attempts, I am trying to kick the tablet habit. This time, however, I have enlisted the help of a counsellor. I have to pay for the privilege, as the NHS does not apply sufficient funds for more than a few sufferers - I understand that my own medical practice can only provide three one-hour sessions per week in total of free counselling, which I would think is a mere token gesture in recognition of the need and barely skims the surface of the problem. I was anyway told by my doctor that the waiting list was so long it was not worth applying. How fortunate I am to be in paid employment, albeit my wife and I qualify for Family Credit.

In the interim between the time of my breakdown and the present day my life and that of my family has not been a bed of roses. Soon after I began to recover I discovered alcohol, a treacherous friend and unforgiving taskmaster with whom I did battle for many years. I was also a heavy smoker for many years and it is not surprising that it took its toll in the form of a heart attack which came four years ago. Surprising myself I was able to kick the smoking habit with ease the very same day as the attack and I haven't smoked since. It must be God having his way with me at last! Thanks also to a great deal of help I have taken no alcohol for the last twelve years - another major miracle in my life!

Yet still I am taking tranquillisers. Because of my depleted confidence I had had to give up a promising career at University and take up work with which I struggled to cope, even though it was below my former ability. Since that time I feel I have never achieved the level of earnings which might have been attainable with a confidence level commensurate with good mental health. The insecurity, anger and depression which were the legacy of my childhood still seemed to be active within me and would erupt with ferocity at times, casting a cloud over my family life and threatening to reproduce in my long-suffering children the very symptoms which had plagued myself for so many years and from which I still could not escape without the aid of medication.

Somehow I know I have to kick the tablet habit if I am ever to find real peace of mind. This time I can see a chink of light at the end of the tunnel, just enough to keep my hopes alive and keep on trying through the pain. At least I am not going it alone this time.

However I fare I hope this brief history of my illness may in some small way help to improve the way forward for others in the future. It is of course easy to be wise after the event and I acknowledge that there are many who must have regular medication for their lives to be at all tolerable. Nevertheless, I feel in my case I have been a victim, like so many, of 'easy option' tablet therapy, which has led to problems capable of remedy being buried for years with all the regrettable consequences of failed potential and diminished lives for the want of proper therapy to address the underlying causes.

Looking back I would say that the quality of my life has been so damaged by the mistaken application of tranquillisers, I would not wish under any circumstance to re-live the greater part of it, and for that I believe I have to thank in part the attentions of the West Suffolk Mental Health Service.

I am too old now to indulge in dreams, but one day when I am well I hope I'll see the truth as it was, the cause of all my pain, and the way it should or could have been in a better more enlightened world.

by Neville Lewis

In Search of A Listening Ear

Everyone wants to tell me their tale of today, but who will listen to mine? Patiently, I listen to every murmur, how they saved on their soap or their wine, how toilet rolls are up in Marks's but down in Gateway, how the cat got lost and was found, their daily ups and downs, their weekly losses and gains...

But now I'm called to see if a compressor's in stock. Ah yes, Joe has spotted it. "Do they want it today?" he asks. "I'm not sure," say I. 'You're not sure?" he says, with that sneering tone of enquiry as though I should know everything, "No, I didn't take the call, but it was either for today or tomorrow. I must go tell Shirley we've got it - she's about to go home." "You must order a replacement," says Joe, rambling on. I manage to get away to tell Shirley. Back upstairs Joe tells me, "We'll also need a Senator condenser - on second thoughts, better let James order that." I mention it would be best to order the replacement compressor at the same time - then comes a worrying thought, who is to remember to tell James all this? Am I supposed to do it or can it be left to Joe? I must be sure in order to avoid the painful recriminations which always accompany failure to read his intention...I manage somehow to get his attention as it darts to and fro and he says we must both remind James the next day...

Having settled that I glance nervously again at the pile of service reports still to be processed into invoices which I had started on three days earlier. Will they never, ever get finished? Now Joe is regaling me with his encounter today with an unusual Caterpiller Crawler which was used to push a lifeboat out to sea. Everyone smiles sympathetically and with interest at the difficulties of the tasks involved as he relates them in detail to his captive audience. Who, I wonder, will listen to my tale of today, or even consider I might have one worth the telling? Grimly I recalled the day I was rash enough to mention to Joe the walk I once did from Bury to Long Melford, only to receive that strange sneering response of amazement and contempt as though I had committed some kind of social solecism or that for anyone to mention an event of such small significance was beyond his comprehension. Again my thoughts turn anxiously to the pile of service reports on my desk and the growing mountain of items to be dealt with after that. How will I ever get it all done, I wonder, knowing that it matters to no-one except myself and my employers whether I manage to cope with it or not!

Rick now exclaims at me while in the corridor that I must order an Eco evaporator fan right away for Van den Burgh. "Joe knows the sort," he assures me. But Joe doesn't know at all when I ask him. "They're all the same, anyway!" exclaims Rick when I consult him again, "like the one we fitted at Sappa!" Fact is when I come to order the part I am assured by our supplier that this isn't the case at all as some models of Eco Cooler do carry different types of evaporator fan, so again I go back to Rick and he then agrees I must phone the company back and get them to obtain the model number of the unit to determine exactly what is required. I begin to wonder who is the engineer and who is doing the accounts...I wonder too on whose shoulders the implacable weight of censure and blame would have fallen had I ordered on the basis of the Sappa fan specification and the item had turned out to be the wrong type, after the memory, integrity and patience of those involved had been tested to the limit at the inevitable interrogation and trial which followed...

"Have you faxed Mercantile yet?," comes a cry from the other office. "Not yet. I'll do it now then," say I. "For heaven's sake," I am thinking, "will no-one ever understand I have my own work to do?" "Must let them see the invoice today if we can," says Neil, "then send a copy in the post." The two of us are now involved searching for the fax number, which at last is found. But something is wrong. I cannot make the fax work. "Check the number," says Neil. I have, of course, already checked it twice. "It's correct," I tell him. "Give them a ring then," says Neil, "to check it with them. I've got the number here somewhere." He passes me the number and I ring the company. They tell me the fax number is correct. Again I try the fax. Again it fails to go through. "Okay," says Neil, "let's try what Joe showed me the other day. Switch the fax to automatic." I switch it to automatic and Neil rings the fax number on line 2. At length it connects and we hear the piercing signal. "Press the green button!" calls Neil. I press the green and the fax goes through. "Can we get a copy in the post?" says Neil. "I'm not doing the post anymore," say I, "frankly it's too much hassle, and no-one ever gave me a word of thanks for doing it anyway..."

"Okay," says Neil, evidently unconcerned.

Now I'm wanted on the mobile by James at Clifton Cars. I'll soon need to leave for my appointment with the doctor, but there is just time. He needs prices of gas and oil and all the workings out to be done (including VAT) as he says he's lost his calculator. If I believe that, I'm thinking, I've definitely lost my marbles! However I hold his hand through that as I did with Neil's fax - two grown men in need of a helping hand! I wonder in all my life who ever held mine!... always just a piece in someone else's jig-saw - my own blown away by the wind all those years ago...

And who will listen to my tale of today when I get home? Again I hear of the special offers, the bargain prices, the latest store starting up, the dress that just won't fit, the tit-bits of gossip going about the town or on the media, all that our sons have done or are doing today, and any new information come to light about our new neighbour to help satisfy my wife's insatiable curiosity. "Oh, and don't forget to put the bin out tonight!" she reminds me as she settles back into her mail-order catalogues in the never-ending quest for the right garments at the right price. All the time the telly is blaring out its strident endless round of mirth and excitement, violence and sex and teasing advertising, often to an empty room when the boys are engaged on the computer, but no-one bothers to turn it off...

I go alone into the garden for a little peace, feeling sad inside at my world and the people in it, so intent on their own affairs I hardly seem to matter to any of them. Is this the final reality I have been seeking, the only real world where no-one cares for anyone but themselves, where I'm just a slave to attend to others' needs while my own are seldom met, and don't seem to merit a moment's thought in anyone else's head...

The birds are twittering in the trees; the swirling clouds roll slowly, silently across the sky; the green meadow unfurls and my eyes come to rest on the pale blue haze of the distant skyline; and God reaches down and holds my hand...

Copies to Neil and Shirley 14.12.96

Dear Joe and Marjorie,

I feel I owe you a little more explanation than I have given so far of my reasons for seeking the help of a counsellor at the present time, especially in order to allay any concerns you may be having at my seeking help of this nature in the first place, also hopefully to dispel any unnerving suspicions that I am indeed some kind of "geriatric junkie" in need of a "fix" every now and then in the loo, which may have entered anyone's mind at the mention of the word "counselling"!!

Although my life in the main has been blessed with a huge amount of happiness and good fortune, I was at the age of 21 in so much pain that I had to be given painkillers by my doctors in order to be able to cope. Although some efforts were made to locate the source of the pain, they had no success, so I was forced to continue with the painkillers in order to stay in work. However there was a drawback in that the pain itself and the side-effects of the tablets I was given have tended to have a disabling effect on my life to the extent that I have always wanted to find the source of the pain and remove the necessity for taking the tablets - which is basically what I am trying to do right now.

by Neville Lewis

By now you may appreciate that the 'pain' I am talking about was and is emotional, not physical, and the painkillers are tranquillisers and anti-depressants as opposed to ordinary analgesics. (I would stress at this point that at no time in my life have I ever been stupid enough to take any illegal drug or narcotic in order to escape the 'pain', and have only ever taken non-addictive medically prescribed drugs as recommended by my doctor.) But for me pain is merely pain in whatever form it comes and I know that my own 'pain' has been disabling for me just as any physical pain can disable, such as the pain in Neil's knee or indeed in Shirley's face.

Having digested that you may well ask why on earth the problem has still not been resolved after all these years! The trouble is that the source of emotional pain is sometimes so deep-rooted and difficult to find that even a full course of 1000 hours of professional psychotherapy can still fail to trace the real cause, let alone provide an effective remedy. As I could never contemplate such treatment for myself for reasons of finance and because I never felt "severely" disabled by the problem, I tried many times instead to 'go it alone' but never met with any success mainly because the pain always became so intense that the likely outcome without the resumption of tablets would have been another breakdown similar to that when I was 21 which knocked me flat for a year. Indeed, my younger brother, who is a medical consultant, warned me some years ago that this would invariably happen unless I was able to find the source of the pain and come to terms with it. However, now that inexpensive treatments such as counselling are more readily available and affordable I have decided to have another go at solving the problem.

This time I believe, by some miracle, I may have found the real source of my "pain" and an effective way of dealing with it. I have taken virtually no tranquillisers since early August, I am no longer on anti-depressants and for the first time in years the pain, which was intense for a time, at last seems to be going of its own accord. I can tell you my feelings of relief at times have been indescribable! Nevertheless I feel even now I cannot be totally sure of the outcome, and I know perfectly well that going back on the tablets is still a possibility which I may have to accept. That's okay, because I know there is always the chance of a breakthrough sometime in the future.

I know there is still much fear and prejudice in many people's minds about the kind of "pain" I am referring to in this letter. There really is no "mystery" about it; in fact it is as common in its varying degrees shapes and forms as the common cold and in most people does not even require any treatment, except maybe a short course of sleeping pills after a bereavement, or perhaps a brief period on anti-depressants after the misery of a divorce with no shoulder to cry on. For this reason I feel entitled to talk about my pain just as freely and unashamedly as Neil might wish to about his knee or Shirley about her face. Nonetheless I prefer not to do so, firstly because most people find these things pretty difficult to cope with however well-intentioned they may be, and secondly because there is no real pleasure for me in recalling or describing my kind of "pain". Occasionally one meets up with someone in everyday life who can cope with and be of real help in such matters, but in my experience such people are very rare indeed, I suppose simply because most of us are incapable of the depth of understanding and compassion required for such a purpose.

As I said earlier, I have been blessed with a great deal of good fortune in my life, and it only remains for me to say I am very pleased I came to work for the company. If you have managed to read through all this to the very end, and without too much embarrassment or distress, may I say a very big "well done!" and thank you for doing so, and I hope you have a very happy Christmas!

To Shirley 23.12.96

You are not going to like me for this, but I cannot let another day pass without expressing some at least of my gratitude for the incredible help you have been to me in finding the source of the emotional pain I have tried to relieve with tablets for so many years. You cannot imagine the intense feelings of joy and relief I have experienced this past week, which has been so much due to the loving support you have given over recent weeks, in between coping with the pressures of your job and caring for the needs of your family.

For most of my time with the company I must admit I was so full of paranoid fears of people and situations that I totally mistook your wonderful directness and honesty for overbearing pride and arrogance. How I could have been so mistaken in a person I shall never know! Thankfully I see you in such a different light now! The night of my dream when I kissed you and amazingly you returned my kiss was, I believe, the turning point in my attitude towards you, and instead of being in such awe, nay fear, of the power of your honesty, I began to feel that here was someone whom I might come to trust, and with whom I could share at least some of my past.

Much of the rest you know. What you do not know is the impact of those few words which you spoke in response to my confession that as a child I had wanted to kill my father, whose behaviour I feared would drive my mother from the family home and so deprive me of the only source of love I had in the world. I cannot remember your exact words, but they were something like, "so like any child would think", and you can have no idea of my feelings on hearing those simple, matter-of-fact words of sympathy and reassurance! They seemed to be spoken with such incredible tenderness, love and compassion that I felt you were actually standing right behind me and trying to reach out and touch me to give me comfort. At the same time I had an overwhelming sensation of being completely enveloped in warmth and love. I also felt strangely aware of the presence of Someone Else in the room watching and caring, yet I was sure there was only you and I there!

You are not going to thank me for this, Shirley, but I've shed buckets of tears since that day every time I have felt that God really does love and care for me, and indeed always has done throughout my entire life, so much so indeed that I can have no choice but to love myself also.

Enough of this! You will want to kick me so hard after hearing all of this that it won't be funny! I will tell you only one thing more - my visit to church was really to offer my thanks for this wonderful experience - but the atmosphere didn't seem quite right and my suspicions were confirmed by the words which later came from the vicar at the pulpit. Anyone who could cheerfully consign all of the world's poor homosexuals to perdition because of a few words in the bible could hardly be expected to feel any sympathy or compassion for someone who had once wished to kill his own father.

When later we shook hands at the church door and he asked me how I had come to be at the service, I felt unable to share any of my experience with him, and simply said I had come to confess my sins.

I think he missed out on a good thing.

Have a fantastic Christmas!

To Will, my counsellor 23.12.96

The most important truth I believe I can learn from this most intense spiritual experience of my life is that to love and value myself I need to feel loved and valued by another human being. I always did believe all through my life that at every crossroads and turning point there has been someone whose love I could depend on to see me through the difficult times, and logically I have always believed that God must love and value all of his creation. But to believe one is loved is one thing, to feel the warmth and strength of another person's love with an intense inner awareness is quite another. It may seem strange that such an awareness may not be easily obtained from those of one's immediate family who have loved and valued us for years, perhaps because of that little voice of doubt which thinks maybe after all we are only "needed" rather than truly loved which can creep into our thinking when we are low in self-esteem. In my case the love I needed came from a most unexpected source and in the most dramatic way one could imagine. I believe I had been waiting all my life to hear those few simple words of understanding and compassion, "so like any child would think", and their impact was overwhelming and enduring.

I have written a great deal about my emotions since the day I first put pen to paper at your request, but there is so much to record on to computer that I shall not be able to complete it all until after Christmas. I enclose two letters, one of which went to Shirley, the other to my employers, Joe and Marjorie. This second letter was written with a good deal of anger aroused by the word "junkie" which happened to pop up at work one day when my counselling was mentioned, although I'm sure with no intention to hurt. But it played on my mind so much that I felt I had to write it. I can tell you it made quite an impact, although in hindsight I wish I hadn't begged quite so hard for sympathy!

When I have completed my writing I will make another appointment to see you, hopefully soon after Christmas. Also I will explain how so much of what has happened has I believe been outside my own control, perhaps the most important of such events being that amazing dream, which cannot have lasted more than a couple of seconds but which changed the course of my life!

I hope you have a very happy Christmas, and thanks so very much for your kind help and support,

by Neville Lewis

I look at my anger

This morning first thing I opened the front door and stepped out straight into a pile of dog-shit on the pavement when I went to bring in the rubbish bin. It lay there in a huge pile and it took a good half-hour to clear it all away. While I was doing so it occurred to me that perhaps it might be a good day to take a look at the "shit" in me, and so it was that I came to take a really good look at my anger which I knew had festered inside me for years. My counsellor asked me to write down my thoughts and feelings during the next few days, so that is what I have decided to do.

I know I am angry. I've been angry as long as I can remember. I've damped it down with depressants, doused it with alcohol, buried it with tranquillisers, camouflaged it with sickly-sweet smiles, grimaced at it, groaned with it and done everything I can to escape it or deny it. But still it keeps coming back. However much I try to love, forgive, smile at, condone, make excuses for or try to forget the bastards who keep putting it there, it still rears its ugly head!

And I've always reckoned that anger is ugly because my father was always angry and that frightened me as a boy. He was arrogant too and that is no mistake. You couldn't argue against him. I remember once he even disputed the spelling of a word in the Oxford English Dictionary! He had some funny notions too. How could learning be of any value, he would argue, when lorry drivers earned more than white collar workers. It would be best if we all became lorry drivers - so I was promised a bicycle if I failed the 11+! He didn't care that I didn't want to be a lorry driver. But I did get to stay on at school in the end because my mother wanted me to "do well". They used to argue like hell over my future so for years I never knew where I was going or where I would end up. My father used to call me "professor" because I always seemed to be day-dreaming. Fact is I was so depressed and punch-drunk with all the arguing that was going on that I was most of the time wondering how the hell I could get away from it all. I was too frightened to run away from home, and I hadn't the courage to stick a knife in my father, the one thing which would have ensured that my mother didn't leave home and so take away the only source of love I had in the world! I felt lonely, frightened, angry and very depressed at times, but no-one seemed to care as long as I kept going to school and chalking up the results. I remember longing for love and affection like it was something that existed in another world and you had to go through a wall of fire and brimstone to get to it! I remember once I went on a scout camp and thrilled to the kiss of a girl from the locality who took a shine to me. For weeks afterwards I longed to go back to see her again but I was that miserable and depressed at the time that I believed she would not have wished to see me. After that every girl I ever fell in love with was to remain in ignorance of my devotion. I simply could not risk the shame and

by Neville Lewis

misery of rejection. Such fragile self-esteem as I had could not have survived the pain of failure!

For that reason I inwardly loathed the sordid sexual exploits of my youth and my father's horrific advice to "find 'em, fuck 'em and forget 'em!" Yet the same man who could say that actually loved music and reading, and sometimes he would talk about his genuine love of nature as well as his pride at having sired six fine sons! Yet outside of home he was a bundle of nerves, terrified of going into a hairdressers for a trim or a shop for a packet of cigarettes!

Meanwhile as I grew into my teens I was sucked more and more into the drive for "success" at school. I was elated by the praise of my teachers and their constant cries of "well-done!" and "keep it up!" Gradually, as my hopes of finding the love I so desperately longed for faded from my horizon, I became more obsessed with my studies and the growing need for "outstanding" successes to compensate for my miserable failure as a social human being. And so I put myself under greater pressure than ever to obtain the approval and praise of my hungry taskmasters, the schoolteachers, who never gave up in their incessant quest for ever-higher levels of achievement.

Looking back I realise now what a hollow, hopeless chase I was engaged in! All I had ever really wanted after all was to be loved, and all the lonely years of striving for the elusive rewards of "success" I was really chasing a mirage, an empty, worthless substitute for love called "glory" or "fame"! For praise and adulation are not love. Fame and success do not achieve love. Output and achievement do not add up to love. To have someone laugh at your jokes is not to be loved. Being nice, kind, cheerful, helpful, caring, considerate, tolerant, patient, loyal, devoted and hardworking - none of these is necessary to be loved. Because to be loved is simply to be deeply and comfortably aware that someone truly cares whether you live or die, whether you are happy or sad, to such an extent that they participate and share in those same feelings of sadness and happiness as they occur and do everything in their power to give comfort when comfort is needed, and above all by their genuine care and concern unmistakeably indicate that their happiness and your own are inextricably intertwined. Such love is natural in parents for their children and is essential for the growth of self-esteem and the ability to give and receive love in later life. Sadly, I now believe that it was the legacy of intense anger generated by the fear of losing my mother's love and wishing to kill my father in order to retain that love, which destroyed any real chance for feelings of love and self-worth to grow within me as a child and into adulthood. I have read that when a situation which threatens a basic need such as a mother's love seems hopeless of remedy, the anger generated can be colossal. And so I believe it was with me as a child of about 12 years, for every time I have focussed on that anger I have been terrified by its intensity, almost as though it had substance and shape and had solidified into a ball of hatred too painful to look upon. I have also read that where hatred exists there can be no room for love - the two simply cannot co-exist, and I know now that I have carried that ball of hatred inside me ever since that time. I also now believe that as long as I have such hatred inside me, and however hard I try to do so, I cannot truly value or love myself with genuine sincerity or deep conviction, and consequently I shall remain uncertain of my ability to give or receive love as freely and unconditionally as any normal, worthwhile human being.

I now believe that it was my attempt to suppress or deny my anger which lies at the heart of the problems I have had with love. I have read that until I can accept and value all my feelings I will be unable successfully to release them, and I will therefore remain at their mercy. Always I have tried to deny my anger, mainly because I was frightened of what I might do with it, and as a result it has always been there, unexpressed and uncompromising like a lowering cloud over my personality. At the same time because I have always denied or suppressed my anger, which is after all a natural human emotion, I have habitually denied many of my own needs, and again as I have read, if I deny my own needs I will inevitably be low in self-esteem. The kind of crazy scenario which has often ensued as a result of this denial runs as follows: If I am criticised unfairly and am high in self-esteem I should immediately spring to my own defence with sufficient anger or annoyance to ensure it does not happen again, at least not for the time being. Usually, however, I have such low self-esteem that when I am unfairly criticised I sometimes actually believe there is a genuine reason for the complaint, even though there is none. I may even be so much in the habit of conceding defeat and accepting the blame on such occasions that I am a natural target for such attacks, which may become so frequent and unbearable that my self-loathing for allowing myself to be so misused may become so strong that I am terrified that one more spark may ignite the explosive anger which lies just beneath the surface awaiting release. The unreleased energy of the intense anger may lead to acute anxiety and depression and such an intense fear of failure may follow that the only way out seems to be to quit the job and make a fresh start somewhere else. I have done this several times during my working life and came very close indeed to quitting my present job for the same reasons a few weeks ago, shortly before enlisting the help of a counsellor. Again as a result of this denial I have been so kicked, pissed on, beaten down, humiliated and generally misused by arrogant employers posing as human beings that it isn't funny. Every time it happens I lose a little more faith in humanity and I withdraw a bit more into myself. I'm sure some employers are so arrogant if you told them

by Neville Lewis

they were God they would believe it! Their general credo for managing their staff seems to be as follows: Praise or appreciation for work well done must never be given, lest any employee comes to think his work to be of such value that he asks for a rise! Regular criticism and suggestions that standards of work are not being maintained will ensure that employees are always aware of their failures and shortcomings so that they are constantly striving like hell to do better. Any thought of letting up on the pressure must be avoided. Even a 99% success in a difficult operation must be regarded as a 1% failure and this made perfectly clear to the persons concerned! If you can survive in such an environment without loss of self-esteem and without going off your trolley I would say you must have been loved to bits as a kid! In my case? - who the hell cares?

If I am to stay sane in this world I have to remember there are no limits to the arrogance of human beings and their mischievous ability to desecrate the truth. Whether the person who wrote on the side of the Titanic "Even God could not sink this ship" ever had his arse kicked or drowned with the rest I shall never know. I expect if he did survive people still doffed their caps at him and said "Better luck next time!"

I know this is all negative as hell and I cannot deny it. It is the same every time I try to come off my tablets. The truth of the matter is I seem to have this terrible fear that somehow I will not come up to scratch, that all my efforts will be to no avail and I will eventually fail. I will be rejected as useless, lose my job, the love and respect of my family, defeated, alone, unwanted and unloved. It is a fear that has haunted me for as long as I can remember, and I cannot find an answer to it. I have this awful awareness that I don't easily generate confidence in other people of my ability to cope, that I must always be trying to prove my value to the people I work for; often I suspect that they are dissatisfied or unhappy with my efforts, that unless I try even harder I will eventually fail to meet their expectations and then they will simply say, "Sorry, we've been patient, but you really aren't up to it. I'm afraid you will have to go!"

If I only had a little encouragement now and again, a tiny word of praise or appreciation, just a word of assurance that everything is alright, I have nothing to fear, they are rooting for me anyway and genuinely pleased to have me. Sometimes I feel like a child with no-one around me to show how they do care and how they will look after me. It's as though I am surrounded by people who are all indifferent to my needs and wholly unaware of my feelings or how alone and vulnerable I am feeling. I want to know that I am safe and there is no need to be frightened any more. I want to know that if I put a foot wrong it won't matter, the people around me are not monsters who will suddenly turn on me snarling, telling me they have seen through the mask, they know now that I am just a worthless snivelling wimp of no real value to himself or anyone else and only fit for the gutter. I do not know how I am to convince myself that I am of value to others or to myself. It is when I am racked with this awful anger that I feel least worthy. It seems while the anger is within me I can feel no love for myself or anyone. It is as though the anger has blocked me off from any feelings of self-worth or self-love. I am at the mercy of an emotion that wants to lash out at everything and everyone in its path, fighting for the right to live, breathe and be loved, shouting and yelling that I am here, I matter and I am hurting inside. I cannot say how I feel, I am not allowed a voice, I am not allowed to be of any value, I am not allowed to shout or scream or complain. I must stay silent. I can only listen. "little boys should be seen but not heard." And anyway, my father always says "silence is golden". I have no voice. It is futile to complain. And anyway I am too frightened. And still he keeps criticising her, complaining at all her efforts. She is so fed up with it, I know. I wonder if she will leave one day. What will become of me? There will be nothing left for me to hold on to. No more hope. Just pain and loneliness, deafening anger and pain and loneliness and no-one to care for or love me in the whole wide world...

SUNDAY
THE DAY I BEGAN TO ACCEPT MY ANGER

Today for the first time in my life I began to accept my anger and the reasons for it. It has been a difficult day, with huge surges of anger interspersed with incredible feelings of joy at the thought that God really does love me. I have begun to talk a lot more to Shirley at work about my past and somehow I feel my future hopes of success are in some way tied in with her and her evident support and willingness to listen with care and concern to what I have to say. She seems to show a warmth and understanding I have never been aware of before, and it is strange that we have both had the nickname "Snowball" given to us in the past. Silly coincidence or something more? - I cannot help wondering and hoping...

All morning I have been wandering around in a daze, my mind going over my childhood and youth again and again, trying to make sense of it all and always wondering how on earth I am going to cope with the ever-increasing anger constantly welling up from within. Also it has occurred strongly to me that every time I experience the anger my sense of self-esteem seems to diminish whereas every time I become aware of feelings of love my sense of my own worth and feelings of well-being increase accordingly. It occurs to me that the only situations

by Neville Lewis

where I have ever been able to release some of my extreme anger were in the family home either at my mother or mother-in-law or at my wife and children, or else at the management team above me at work where I was once protected by a very strong union and almost any kind of abuse was tolerated by the people in charge. In all these cases the innocent victims had no real power of retaliation so it was safe for me to deliver my venom with impunity. I take no pride or comfort from knowing that I have abused those I love so abominably in this way; all I can say in my defence is that I knew my anger once released was so out of control it would have backfired on me with awful effect had it been directed at anyone capable of hitting back. Consequently most people I have known during my life have been blissfully unaware of the anger which has always lurked beneath the impenetrable facade of good-natured bonhomie which I skilfully perfected over the years, to such an extent that I even came to believe myself at times that this was the real "me"! I remember asking my first psychiatrist after several months of treatment for the anxiety and depression which hit me when I was 21, what sort of a person she thought I really was. Her answer was "a thoughtful, loving sort of person", which spoke volumes for my ability as an actor, even during a state of near breakdown, to hide from view the anger underneath the facade, and I remember how my younger brother collapsed with laughter on hearing such a misstatement of my true nature. In later years I came to loathe myself for the extreme lengths of people-pleasing to which it seemed necessary to resort to maintain acceptable relationships with friends and with colleagues at work. One man who befriended me for a while told me without compunction that I was "obsequious, patronising and sycophantic" and that in truth I did not have to be like that, but I could never see any possible way of changing such pathetic, demoralising behaviour.

Around lunchtime I was wandering around a shop near my home, trying to remember what I had come to purchase with my mind still fixed on my past, when it suddenly occurred to me with great force that I had never fully accepted my anger as being a natural, necessary part of my make-up as a human being and as integral to me as a person as any of the emotions with which I am endowed. It was as though for the first time the anger I had carried with me all those years, instead of being something alien and unfriendly, like some kind of transplant which my body refused to accept, all at once slotted like a piece of a jigsaw into its proper, natural allotted place in the scheme of things as though it had merely been waiting all that time only for my consent to do just that. Yet the moment it happened I knew somehow there and then that from now on my anger would no longer be the terrible problem it had been for so long, and it was with a huge sense of relief at a great burden having been lifted at last that I left the shop and made my way home! As I came to my front door I drew a picture of my father in my mind's eye and saw myself insert a knife into his body. I felt at once a sense of relief followed by a feeling of deep sadness, but no guilt or remorse. At last he was gone and I could begin to let go of my anger.

At this point in my story I must mention the importance to me of one phone-call which I made to the Suffolk Health Authority, the same day that I first contacted my counsellor, Will. The call was made in anger at the evident lack of financial support offered by the Health Service to cover the cost of counselling for people such as myself, desperately trying to withdraw from tranquillisers in order to obtain an acceptable quality of life - (I had just been told by my GP that they were taking no more applications for free counselling for the time being as the waiting list was so long!). By amazing good fortune I was transferred to a man who was able to give me the phone number of an organisation in my home town who could help me lobby for more support for my cause, and who call themselves the "Survivors of Mental Health Services in West Suffolk". By an even greater stroke of good fortune when I visited their office a few days later and told one of their staff something of my story, the lady concerned, to whom I shall always remain indebted, immediately recommended for my attention the book which has been such a huge help to me in recent weeks, the "Self-Esteem Workbook" by Lynda Field. Having read a few extracts from their copy of this book I decided to go out and buy a copy for myself. I must say it has been of inestimable value to me in helping me come to terms with my emotions, especially my anger, of which I was so frightened for so many years. Perhaps the most valuable statements for me were that I need to "love and value all my feelings" and that "when you can love and value yourself - whatever you may be feeling - you will no longer be at the mercy of your emotions." This most important book with its words of wisdom has helped me in many ways which tie in with the help I've also been getting from Will, and I do believe that without it I would never have got this far on the road to recovery.

MONDAY
SUDDENLY COMES THE SUN!

At last now I am beginning to smile through the tears! Today has been an incredible day after a very painful week-end. I remember saying to Shirley soon after she arrived at work that I reckoned I "knew where I was coming from" and she laughingly replied that she rather wished she "knew where she was going to", although on reflection she "wasn't so sure"! I am fairly sure that it was this day that I experienced the wonderful, incredible awareness of God's love for me as expressed through Shirley and as described in my letter to her a few days later. The following is what I wrote later the same night as I rested in bed.

by Neville Lewis

Today for the first time in a very long while I have had in some degree a feeling of real peace of mind, a real sense of relief at having a burden lifted and some feelings of real happiness which are coming to me even as I write. However, I have not slept this night because I seem to have all these urgent emotions coming up at me, needing to be examined and assessed to see where they belong in the scheme of things and why they are there! - and always in the front of the array, demanding and insisting on being recognised and accepted, the one I fear the most, the tyrant anger. Sometimes I wonder whether my heart will hold out under the strain and I can only pray that it does! In the end, around 6am, I have had to take a tranquilliser even though I hated doing it. But my thoughts and emotions gradually subsided enough to enable me to sleep, for two hours at any rate, which is better than none at all.

TUESDAY

Today, Tuesday, has been one of the hardest days of my life. Throughout the day I have seemed to swing like a pendulum from a state of near panic to feelings of being really confident, assertive and in control. At times I was so unsure of my ability to concentrate enough to cope with my work that I had to keep reminding myself of a poem I once had to recite to the whole school in front of all the teachers and governors when I was a boy, John Milton's sonnet "On His Blindness". I remembered it going as follows, and its words gave me comfort: "Does God exact day labour, light denied?" I fondly ask. But Patience, to prevent that murmur, soon replies, "God doth not need either man's work or his own gifts; who best bear his mild yoke, they serve him best: his state is kingly. Thousands at his bidding speed, and post o'er land and ocean without rest. They also serve who only stand and wait." It didn't matter, I thought, whether I was able to cope with my job or not; even if I was to break down completely as I did at the age of 21, I would still have God's love wherever I went, whatever my status or role in life - "they also serve who only stand and wait." In fact this conviction has been growing and giving me comfort all day, the realisation that God's love has never failed me and never will! It occurred to me strongly that my mother never did leave home when I was a child, and her love was there for me for many years to come. When I was 12 she was just 49 years old. She never did leave the family home, and she lived to be 91! It also occurred to me that at every stage of my life there had always been someone who cared for me and gave me their friendship and support. The love of these friends I made along the way had always been there to help me through and give me the strength to carry on when my spirits were low. Not least among those who really cared for me was my own mother-in-law, who in my stupid arrogance I sometimes "looked down on" for her lack of education and her "common" manner of speaking. Yet during the worst of my drinking days she looked after me like a second mother, waking me every morning with a cheery smile and a cup of tea and seeing to my every need without complaint and taking my anger on the chin again and again without any aggression in return. Her daughter Mary, whom eventually I married, has no GCSE's, no qualifications, only a sensitive enquiring mind and a huge fund of patience and love. For love has no need for qualifications or degrees, no need of learning or diplomas and has no ambition for money or status. It flows like a stream straight from Heaven, and that flow I am sure now will never cease, because God with his love will always be there for me. The one ingredient which I realise now has always been missing from my life has been that of faith, faith that, come what may, God's enduring love would see me through all the difficult times. The fact is I have had the most incredible good fortune in my life, despite often abominable behaviour towards those who have loved me. Yet always I have felt pursued and bedevilled by fear, full of anxiety that somehow I shall be unable to cope and no-one will want to know me or give me love. Now at last I feel truly aware of God's enduring, never-failing love, and I cannot hold on to my crazy fears any longer. I feel so good right now it's unbelievable!

It is now 6.45 Wednesday morning. I did manage to sleep last evening from 7 till 11 but I have not slept since. It's okay because I am at peace and I know now that God's love will never fail me. Who could have thought that the very person with whom I shared the office and who's incessant talking seemed to pose the greatest threat to my ability to cope, would prove to be my greatest friend in my time of need, who would be such a willing listener, and who would share my faltering steps to self-discovery with such deep compassion and understanding. Nothing could surpass the feelings of joy and relief I have felt this night! This has been the hardest day yet the happiest night of my entire life!

WEDNESDAY

Today I have amazed myself by two things which I have been able to do fearlessly and spontaneously which would have been impossible before this week-end. Firstly I have been able to express mild anger in a useful and positive way on two occasions. I became irritated with the persistence of a salesman who was trying to sell something we might not need and which I had no authority to order, and I finally said with an edge in my voice and some degree of firmness, "If I find when you come on Friday that I can have some of those items then I will, but I cannot give you any guarantee." It was said with just enough asperity to make the salesman look and note my expression, and he at once stopped his pestering. Also I was able to castigate Shirley for failing to see her doctor about a cough which she has had for some time and which sometimes makes her feel dizzy. I insisted she should see him at once. Then when she complained about the cost of prescriptions I gave her such a withering look and such a fierce reprimand that she agreed with a laugh that she would indeed go to see him after all.

Another unusual thing which happened today was that for once I stood up for someone in their absence in the face of opposition from those around me. We have a new manager who is a little unpopular only because, as I put it to the others, he is merely seeking to "establish his authority." I was able to make some of the others see the sense of what I had been saying - so I stood up for my convictions for once instead of just going along with the crowd and risking being two-faced as a result. It made me feel good about myself and I believe I earned some respect for the stand I made from the others. All this was very unusual for me, so it really has been an incredibly good day.

Most amazing of all, this has all been happening to me without my having to think or deliberate at all beforehand! So often in the past I have been racked with anxiety as to how my actions or words might be received. It is almost as though my role has changed completely from being a puppet pulled by strings to being for once under my own control, from being a zombie subdued by drugs to someone who has suddenly come alive! And now that the deep-rooted fear and anger from the past is recognised and being dealt with, the desperate need to pretend has gone and I can be me!

THURSDAY

Today has been another good day even though my new-found self-esteem has faltered a little at times. I realise that it will need to be nurtured and protected as I go along. I have to remain aware, if I do slip back now and again into old ways of thinking, that no matter what happens I am of real worth, I am of value. On one occasion I started to get a bit panicky and began running around like a headless chicken trying to cope with half a dozen tasks at once! But it's okay because I know where I'm coming from and that I don't have to keep bending double or tear myself apart in an insane effort to meet impossible demands. All I or anyone can do is one job at a time and there is no reason on earth to think that I should expect more of myself than that. So I did manage to slow down, regain my composure and think well of myself again. I feel I have got through a lot today, but although I am pleased with myself I realise I don't have to be over-pleased, as though I had achieved something unusual or extraordinary. Gradually I am coming down to right-size and a proper perception of my real worth and capability as a human being. Above all I know I can be loved for myself, and that more than anything else constitutes all I need for true happiness and to feel that life is really worthwhile, not just something to be endured. I have been searching my bible recently for that brief chapter about charity, i.e. love, and today I managed to find it, and the following piece now has greater relevance and meaning for me than ever before in my life:

"And though I have the gift of prophecy, and understand all mysteries, and all knowledge; and though I have all faith, so that I could remove mountains, and have not charity, I am nothing."

14.9.97

BOSS	Where the heck have all the line tap valves gone?
ME	*You expect me to know?*
BOSS	Well, Yes.
ME	*Then you hold me accountable for all movements of stock out of the store?*
BOSS	Of course - you're the storeman.
ME	*With four keyholders with free access at any time?*
BOSS	Er...
ME	*Thinks, Gee, I must be God...*

~

BOSS	Why ever did you order that, I've got loads of them in my van!
ME	*I didn't know.*
BOSS	Why didn't you ask me first then - Ive told you before I don't want anything ordered without my knowledge!
ME	*Well, er, we did try to reach you on Band 3 but you were out of range.*
BOSS	Why didn't you try the mobile?
ME	*Well, to be honest we didn't think it worth it as the item only cost 3 pounds.*
BOSS	3 pounds is still 3 pounds and it's my money so next time use the mobile.
ME	*What if we only need a 50p bolt from B and Q and you're in Christchurch?*
BOSS	(Silence - no reply)
ME	*Thinks, Christ, he's stopped, I must be God!*

~

by Neville Lewis

BOSS   I see you ordered some copper tube on Friday - what was that for?
ME   *Well, we had none at all in the store and the engineers were all saying they have hardly any pipe on any of the vans so it seemed the sensible thing to do at the time.*
BOSS   Well, I've got plenty on my van - it's a pity you didn't wait till I got back or at least wait till the end of the month.
ME   *Thinks... slap wrist, naughty boy, I should have known he would see it different... I must be God!*

ME   *Thinks - If I don't soon become God I'm never gonna cope with this job!*

~

BOSS   Why did you order that without telling me - I think I've got 2 or 3 somewhere at Whittlesfield.
ME   *(Thinks,... if you don't know for sure I don't think even God would if it's at Whittlesfield). (Aloud): I guess we didn't expect you to have one - it's an unusual item.*
BOSS   Not really, I remember using one 4 years ago...
ME   *(Thinks... pity really I'm not God. Though I'm not so sure, cos he works for nothing - at least I get a wage, even if I don't deserve it with so little knowledge of what's required...*

9.10.97

Can it be wise to use phrases like "sink or swim", "success or disaster", and "academic suicide", all of which were recently used by speakers at an information session for parents at one of our schools, in order to induce fear of failure as a motivating force in the obsessive drive for maximum performance in our schools?

I do not think so. I believe fear to be a two-edged sword which can reap a terrible harvest of misery and pain if, as often it can, it breeds the lunatic notion that success at this time in such limited, arbitrary aims is vital and essential to "success" in later life. True, the words were directed at the parents, not the children. Nonetheless substantial advice was given at the meeting on schemes and strategies to deal with and alleviate as far as possible any "anxiety" or "worry" which the child might well feel at times with so much pressure on him to perform well, which could harm the whole process and reduce his chances for ultimate success, especially at a time of acknowledged "insecurity" in his life. So fear, and paradoxically fear of fear, seem to be accepted as necessary ingredients in the drive for optimum success. My feelings on the matter are simple enough: would a trainer put down his dog just because it failed to go through the hoops first time out in the ring? Furthermore, would he think it useless or worthless even if it never managed any of the hoops, contrary to every hope and expectation of success? I do not think so. He might even love it all the more for its lack of ability, which is perhaps more than can be said for the way we treat some of our children, or indeed our partners, when they fail to meet our expectations!

The truth I have found is that unreasonable, excessive fear is by far the most damaging commodity I can receive into my life. Every time I have allowed it in - and who, especially a child, is strong enough to withstand the pressures, often subtle and unseen, which introduce it - it has brought a measure of of pain which takes away something of the "joy of living" which was my birthright as a child, and so reduces the quality of my life. As fear comes to dominate more and more of my life, the less I am actually able to cope, until the fog descends and thickens to such a degree that life for many becomes a grim ordeal, a burden to be borne in silence and alone.

At the same time I know that my relationships with others have frequently been damaged and distorted by anger, irritability, guilt, distrust, self-loathing and depression, all arising one way or another from this terrible burden of fear which I believe is due more than anything to my conditioning by a society which induces blinkered, self-centred aims with obsessive zeal and intensity, focussing solely on the merits of personal proficiency and success. I believe this obsessive self-seeking, fear-driven quest for "success" conflicts with and denies my basic need as a human being to be able to love and care for others, without expectation of return, without which any genuine and lasting happiness is quite beyond reach. It is hardly surprising perhaps, in view of the myopic, impoverished values which society seems to consider sufficient for our needs, to learn that more than three million people in our society are receiving treatment for depression at any one time!

A few weeks ago a friend of mine happened to mention that while she was waiting in a doctor's surgery she heard someone ask a little girl what she was thinking. Almost at once, the little girl replied, "I love my Mummy." My friend admitted that tears sprang to her eyes as she acknowledged the wonderful beauty and truth of those few simple words.

by Neville Lewis

The truth is so simple we seldom see it. The fact that love is the most natural, the most nourishing, the most satisfying, the most rewarding and the most valuable feeling known to man is set aside, lost and forgotten in the mad, self-centred scramble for more and more of the so-called "good" things of life, money, possessions, power and social status, with an almost demonic focus on the drive for greater output and efficiency in almost every aspect of our lives!

The simple truth, that I myself am only now beginning dimly to perceive, is that we must somehow break free from the prison of fear in which society seems to think we should live, and allow love back into our lives, if we are ever to experience again something of the joy of living and the radiant beauty of the world we live in, which we all knew and were aware of as children. For thankfully, after much pain and misery and a great deal of wrong thinking, I have been fortunate enough to obtain a new awareness of these things and a new perspective on my life which is unbelievably better and worthwhile than anything I have known before.

Finally I must repeat the truth I have found in my life, that fear takes away my ability to love others as it focuses my thoughts more and more on myself and my self-centred cravings and needs, until ultimately I come to despise and to hate myself and everyone else who share my joyless existence. But love can restore me to sanity as can nothing else, and only love can bring me out of the Hell that for many years is the only reality many people know. I also now believe that, paradoxically, only love, the opposite of fear, can release my full potential and bring me the happiness and joy of living which I believe to be God's intention and wish for every human being.

13.11.97

Sailors have a rum do at times! Take poor Neil for example, trying so hard to keep a tight ship with everything secure and battened down for a safe voyage and a well-disciplined crew to ensure the ship doesn't founder or run aground.

First he has Admiral Nelson to contend with who seldom sees eye to eye with his plans and at the drop of a hat will force him to tack or turn about, sometimes making him take a risky passage through narrow straights with torn and tatty rigging and ropes and halyards that have seen better days...

Then there's the cunning bosun who has steered his own course at his own discretion and at his own speed for as long as anyone can remember and has never yet obeyed an order from the bridge without questioning its wisdom or practicality, nor failed to declare a job impossible if it might require a little extra time on deck to complete it...

Then there's the excellent but garrulous cook, a redoubtable lady indeed whom nobody dares defy, not even the admiral, except for the luckless cabin-boy who challenged her power, only to fall victim to her spell and to flee mumbling below decks, overwhelmed by the torrent of words which threatened to capsize the ship completely. Occasionally he emerges briefly to scream abuse at the captain and crew before withdrawing quickly below, fearfully praying he won't be thrown overboard for his temerity!

Meanwhile the rest of the motley crew, unused to discipline, restless at times and looking for trouble, reluctantly yield to Neil's command. And Neil, with furrowed brow and uncertain at times, holds nonetheless on to the wheel and keeps the ship on course...

Fearful of being too kind, even to the cook, having witnessed the fate of the poor cabin boy, like all good mariners he clings to the hope that somehow courage and discipline will see them through and bring them home to the happy harbour every sailor longs to see...

(Neil, of course was the firm's manager, the Admiral the boss of the outfit, the cook the garrulous, formidable female I fell in love with, while I was the luckless cabin boy in charge of the accounts and ordering of spare parts for the engineers.)

RATS

Rats - all of 'em! Just look at them scurrying for more rat money, more rat possessions, more rat territory! They'd rip granny rat's throat if they thought they'd benefit - or put her in a rat home to rot so long as it left them free to make more rat money or go on more rat holidays! That's the same as ripping her throat only more slowly, more painfully!

I've seldom seen two of them hug each other in friendship, but I've seen 'em smile sweetly lots of times except when their rat security or their rat vanity was threatened - then they bare their teeth and show a different face to their fellow rats, who withdraw in silence until bold enough to try again. In my whole life I can only recall one hug in friendship and love from a fellow family rat - that was from my

by Neville Lewis

brother rat after his wedding, when for a moment he seemed to become human. It quite took me aback, I can tell you, but I think he soon reverted to kind as I understand most of his rat output and enterprise now goes into improving his rat home!

When I was a kid I was told by my rat Mum that love could wait - meanwhile she said I had such rat promise it would be a waste not to put every rat effort into becoming a somebody rat, and to put every ounce of energy into making something of my rat self and the most of my rat talents - whatever that was all supposed to mean! After I had achieved rat success she and her friends could all jump up and down in rat excitement at such a wonderful rat achievement, then having tired of that they could turn away and focus their rat attention on something more rat interesting, like having a cup of rat tea and criticising and condemning the rat world in general for all its wicked ways, and the lack of rat care and rat understanding in rat society today!

Meanwhile, just as I was being told that rat love could wait, my rat Mum was becoming so annoyed with my rat Dad, who was a real hard rat with a loud rat temper, that she sometimes threatened to leave the rat home for good. I guess as she was the only real source of rat love I knew at the time, I began to wonder whether I would ever get enough to survive, and so I began to make desperate efforts at school to achieve the rat success my rat Mum wanted for me in order to make her stay.

Yet always I knew deep down that my efforts could never be sure of success, and so fear of failure grew gradually into such a monster within that finally I succumbed and slipped into a state of deep rat depression.

I am married now with my own little rat home and rat wife and family, whom sadly I have rat terrorised for years with the same fears, anger and depressions which were the legacy of my rat childhood. My poor rat wife has only felt able to say once that she 'loved' me and that was only because she was terrified at the time that I was about to desert her and leave the rat family home, while my eldest son had his own generous offer and declaration of love rejected out of hand, partly because I was in such a foul mood at the time, but mostly because, I guess, I had no knowledge or experience of how to handle such a wonderful offer!

This last rat year I have tried to come off my rat tablets which I've taken for many rat years to help deaden the pain of longing for love and the fear of losing the love that I have. But once again I am feeling my rat pain at this mad rat world, and my rat depression is beginning to take hold once again. My rat job is beginning to get me down and my rat colleagues just don't seem willing to give me the rat support I need to cope, only mushy rat sympathy as I begin to weaken like the rat tears they shed at the end of a sad film prior to switching off and joining their rat friends for a pint or a romp at the local club, or a game of rat bowls on the green.

It's strange, but the one thing I reckon might help is the one thing I know I'll not get from them - and that's a few rat hugs now and again from someone who cares just enough to move on from pity to love and make me feel human again. But I know that's an impossible rat dream in the world of rats as it is, for as Jonathan Swift, the author of Gulliver's Travels, wrote at the beginning of that book, "Human beings are the vilest race of vermin that ever crawled upon the face of the earth!"

24.1.98
Vision of life and the inhabitants of my lonely world

Even as a young boy I can remember wondering if one day I might go insane. Often I would lie awake at night, my thoughts racing frantically like demons through my head, wishing fervently I could get to sleep and knowing how difficult always it seemed to be to get up in the morning, when somehow the world outside and all its terrors had to be faced, my stomach writhing at the prospect and rebelling at any thought of breakfast.

Out there was this crazy world of horrible, yelling, screaming kids who took such a pleasure in pushing, jostling, fighting, teasing and rebuking one another. How could they behave like that, I used to think, with so little care or consideration for others, in such an ill-mannered, unruly, ignorant and boisterous manner, as if they owned the bloody playground, racing around in such a senseless, stupid state of excitement as though that was the only thing they could think of worth doing with their stupid lives.

How could people be like that, I used to think, so indifferent to all the misery and pain there was in the world. Was not this place where we live and everyone in it is rotten to the core, with everybody, including my own mother and father, always angry at one another, always making out how right and how wonderful they all fuckin' were, how they knew everything and you knew fuckin' nothing! Didn't they know I didn't need all this shit in my life, all the yelling, all the fuckin' arguing and shouting and screaming?
All I could think of doing when the arguments really got going at home was to get

right out of the fucking place and go for a bloody good walk in the country! Somehow then the anger and misery inside my head used to gradually go away, I could leave the world behind and mercifully be at peace with nature and with myself, at least for a while. There was something special and soothing about the world of nature, this kingdom where you were seldom disturbed by anyone or anything tangibly frightening or threatening, where often the only sound you could hear was the whisper of your own breath, the gentle gurgling of a stream, the twittering of the birds or the occasional rush of a rabbit or hare which was briefly there and then gone, the soothing silence returning as before to still my thoughts and calm my angry spirit, almost as though God was somewhere here amongst these trees and meadows, even though I knew there was no way HE could really help because He was too remote and anyway HE must be concerned with more important things than to have time for one little chap like me! And anyway it would have taken a miracle to change anything for the better in my life, and everyone knew that miracles only happened in the Bible and there was no real evidence even then, apart from hearsay, that such things had actually taken place, and in any case all that happened centuries ago and very little had happened since and nothing you could really prove!

The world of nature was my only real refuge away from the pain in my world, apart from church which I was forced to attend once every week because they said I had such a fine singing voice, and it would be such a shame to waste it while it was there! And so I sang at services, weddings, funerals, sometimes even solo which made me feel mighty proud and mighty important - at least for the moment! And how wonderful it was to receive the praise and the thanks of the grateful recipients of my singing, so angelic, so fine and so divine as they assured me it was! And I used to go away with my ears still buzzing with the sound of their acclamations and my crazy head swelling with dreams of future glory and even greater and more resounding acclamations and acknowledgements of the wonder of this mellifluous voice of mine! For a while as I walked away from church it seemed a better world, a world of promise and hope that I was walking in, a world that was cleaner and fresher, where the taste of misery and fear had receded from my lips, at least for a while...

All too soon the vision of hope seemed to fade, as once again the darkness closed in on my mind, and I was faced again with the world out there, small, frail and defenceless as I was, the smallest boy for Christ's sake in my fucking class, hardly capable of standing up to a pint-sized girl, let alone any of the vicious bastards of my own sex who prowled the playgrounds and the alleyways around my home in search of anyone smaller and weaker they could tease or annoy at their leisure!

How I would like to have smashed their ugly fuckin' faces in till the blood ran free and they fell to the ground, groaning and grimacing in agony, begging for mercy, pleading helplessly and hopelessly in pain and fear until with a final, vicious, punishing blow I struck and took them totally out of my life and out of their own so I would never ever be bothered by them again!

9.3.98
by John Powell

"Psychologists, in studying human motivation, have found that positive reinforcements of the will, (reward for good conduct) are infinitely more effective than negative reinforcements (punishment for bad conduct). To be constantly critical of a person is obviously a dangerous thing. It tends to undermine his confidence and make all authority obnoxious. However, if one takes the approach of positive reinforcements, tending to overlook small failures in conduct but never failing to recognise and reward (at least with a kind word) the desired conduct, the effect will be almost magical. It is an illustration of the power released in the creation of good self-image. Most people will be in their conduct what we tell them they are."

I therefore now unreservedly acknowledge and accept that any knowledge of computing I may have had which I considered might be of value to the company is actually of no worth or value whatsoever, as indeed was acknowledged right from the start when such a joke was made for so long over the fact that computer stock levels seldom corresponded with the actual, despite repeated and earnest attempts on my part to explain why such a reality was incapable of achievement without a lot more effort and expense. Unfortunately, nobody would take the trouble to sit down and LISTEN, except when they wanted HELP!

Dear Joe and Marjorie

I am writing this to explain as best I can my feelings with regard to my position in the company and my ability to function and cope effectively with the tasks assigned to me.

My main role or task at present is of course accounts, with which I feel I can cope reasonably well. To date my experience of this has been confined to general company accounting up to trial balance, with the production of regular monthly reports which I introduced on my own initiative in order to give a fair indication of how the company was doing on the basis of monthly profit/loss statements.

by Neville Lewis

I regret I am not very knowledgeable at all in areas such as the preparation of final accounts or statutory regulations, nor in general on specific areas of company law and taxation, which of course is a large and complex subject in itself, nor have I any experience of auditing.

I have a little knowledge of computing, which of course is so vast a subject that not even Bill Gates, dare I say, incredibly gifted as he is, could ever hope to know all the varied functions and potential applications of every section or module of every programme on the market.

Indeed I discovered long ago that it is virtually impossible to make any sensible or wise choice for any purpose for any company in terms of software or hardware without the aid of a trusted consultant, some of whom themselves may not be too reliable when it comes to obtaining the right advice. I well remember when I did my course at the college that one lecturer said he knew of several people who on the basis of mischievous or mistaken advice had gone out and bought expensive machines with just enough RAM to load Windows but insufficient memory remaining to run any Windows-based applications, so that effectively they were left with a useless product, rather like building a garage for a car or van with less than an inch either side available for driver or passenger access! (If you need to be enlightened, RAM simply stands for "random access memory", which is the internal, temporary space within the computer "memory store" while it is switched on and which is measured in "bytes" (one byte being the space taken up by one letter of the alphabet or two numeric digits), as opposed to the external, permanent memory which is resident on floppy or hard discs on to which information may be transferred from the internal memory for future use. I only mention this very simple basic principle to illustrate if I can how very difficult it is to explain in layman's terms to anyone not familiar with all the jargon or concepts involved to give easily-understood answers for every step which has to be made to accomplish any computer project.) I myself have always relied on John for support, first because his prices are reasonable, and also he is always willing to help, much like you yourself Joe with our own customers, with any problem whatsoever or, if he cannot help, point me in the right direction. The other day, when as you know the printing of the price list for Marjorie stopped half-way through, after considering the problem, and after his first ideas had been tried with no success, John then suggested Sage might find the answer more readily, which ultimately they did. As it happened it was quite an unusual occurrence, being a hidden bug in the report programme I had written for the print-out, which Sage checked as being okay in principle, but which I was obliged to delete and rewrite again under another filename, with the same criteria and parameters, which this time ran and worked okay. In addition John is local, and can often call in at the office on his way home or whatever to drop anything off or help with a pressing problem which may not be desperately urgent but which perhaps requires a few minutes "on site" at the computer to sort as and when he can. I know he does not always turn up on the day as promised, but I do know I can rely on him totally when the chips are down (sorry for the pun!) to get me out of a jam if I am really out on a limb and in desperate need of help. To be truthful I cannot talk highly enough of the man, because on top of everything else he is pleasant, unassuming, always reassuring and helpful, always willing to help wherever he possibly can with regard to matters of cost, and he never makes a drama out of a crisis, and frankly I consider myself very fortunate indeed to have had the privilege of knowing and receiving the committed support of such a likeable, talented and genuinely helpful and well-intentioned person!

Of course, as I have said, my own experience of computing is very limited, and like everyone else I have to be open to suggestions and advice from others who may be able to help in aspects or areas I have not dealt with before, such as the proposed adaptation of the SOP (Sales Order Processing) module of Sage accounts which certainly should give more efficient and more effective control of the works operation and stock movements, together with the usual time-saving benefits and spin-offs such systems provide.

Now that I have been given the delightful task of turning my incredibly rash suggestion, so unwittingly drawn out of me by our friend Jeremy of dubious parentage, into a reality, I am once again faced with another no-man's land where I have not ventured before, together with the usual uncertainties we all feel when treading new ground and the appropriate path through the minefield of obstacles and blind alleys has to be found to achieve success. I have established from John that others have used this module in similar fashion with the use of product codes to control the works operation, and through Sage I have also contacted a software company who have written an add-on programme compatible with Sage Financial Controller for the same purpose, which is currently available for 600.00 pounds. But they did also confirm John's information that the SOP module can be adapted for this purpose, although as companies grow in size they generally find the programme they themselves have devised is more appropriate to their needs. So my idea is nothing new. All it requires is a pathway through the minefield which is probably no big deal even for me, provided I can be left to take the necessary steps with my own personal mine detector which is unique to me and made up from a compilation of my own personal knowledge and experience of accounts and computing over the past ten years, such as it is. Anyone else's mine detector,

by Neville Lewis

unfortunately, is of no use because I have no access to it. If within the company there is someone better equipped or qualified to deal with the matter I am very willing to forfeit this wonderful opportunity I have of falling on my face and showing what an ass I can be with my mouth!

If however, I am required to do the job I must in any event have the full use of my personal mine detector, which to be fair has to include access as usual to John's good advice, which I have come to rely on over the years as being absolutely sound and dependable, and which has got me out of many a deep hole in the past. So any heavy-handed or misguided attempt to force me at this stage of proceedings to seek out another consultant, or to suggest that my judgement in these matters is unsound or of little value is basically of no help to me whatsoever, and far from being of help only serves to cut the ground from under my feet by diminishing my morale and reducing whatever motivation I may have had in the first place to achieve success almost to the level of zero.

I would make one further point clear. To my way of thinking we can all be wise after the event, and I know we all do it, myself included, especially when other people's decisions or actions have unfortunate repercussions for ourselves. How often I have groaned at my wife, when upset or in low spirits, with such words as, "Why the devil didn't you know we were out of milk? Couldn't you be bothered to look in the ruddy fridge? Now I suppose I've got to go out and get some myself!" I think we've all been there one time or another. But at least, it is to be hoped, we make up for it at other times with some simple word of gratitude or encouragement in response to efforts or actions on our behalf, such as "That was a nice meal," and sometimes just a plain "thanks a lot" can make a cold room feel a good deal warmer! Not that such positive affirmations of a person's value or worth as a human being are very commonplace in the workplace of today. But if I go out and get some coffee from Sainsburys on a Saturday for 3.50 and my wife says on the following Monday she has seen the self-same product marked up in Tesco's for a pound less, and every week that I do the shopping it is pointed out that some product or another could on investigation have been purchased for less from another shop, I would either begin to feel seriously concerned as to my ability to cope successfully with the shopping, albeit by now my wife must surely know I take as much reasonable care as I can to stretch our money as far as it will go, or else eventually I must tell her to go do the shopping herself!

I suppose that's about where I am right now with the company and the latest task I have been given. I know I am not perfect and like everyone else I know am frequently wrong. I know too that in anger or frustration I can sometimes come out with pretty blunt and sometimes hurtful remarks, and I am sincerely sorry for any harm I may have done in this way to you Joe or indeed to anyone else in the company in the past. But if I am to be of any real value to the company I must be allowed sufficient faith and trust in my own judgement, which inevitably comes from my own personal knowledge and experience, to be able to cope successfully with any of the problems involved in the proposed computer scheme, so that I may at least be spared the need to backtrack constantly and to justify decisions I have made in the past which may or may not in hindsight have turned out for the best, and hopefully also be free from the burden of having to provide superfluous and tiresome explanations to someone who is not used to computing or computer terminology, before even the new computers have arrived and before even I have found my way around Windows 95 and the new Windows-based software which is a much more recent, more enhanced version of Sage than the one we use at present.

If I am to continue with my current work for the company I therefore feel I must have some assurance that my judgement will be respected and trusted in regard to the work I am trying to do, and that I will be left alone to work as best I can for the benefit of the company without any further unnecessary and inappropriate interventions or discouragements. If no such assurance can be given, I will with regret be obliged to leave the company and seek employment elsewhere. My hope is that I can continue to work with you, but if attitudes remain the same as well they may despite this letter, I shall have no option but to go. I hope I have given no offence in writing this letter, as certainly none is intended. My greatest difficulty throughout my life has been to communicate my feelings or needs effectively in any face-to-face encounter or confrontation, and when the odds seem stacked against me I either tend to crumble and withdraw or else, these days at any rate, go way over the top in anger, neither of which approach I have to admit is very successful - hence this letter. I can only account for such silly behaviour from the fact that I was very small and fearful as a boy so that whenever angry or provoked I usually tried to hide or suppress my annoyance through fear of reprisal - discretion being the better part of valour! - to such an extent that the habit of appeasement and withdrawal became the habit of a lifetime, while those closer to home and more vulnerable were exposed to a somewhat different and less agreeable image and behaviour. Perhaps it all stems from the fact that my parents insisted on naming me after Neville Chamberlain!

Sometimes it is difficult to see the truth even when it is there in front of your eyes. Nothing especially can be more frustrating or more sickening to have to put up with the unreasonable interference and demands of someone who in spite of claims to the contrary has no real knowledge or experience in an area where you have spent literally years of painstaking effort learning as much as you can to obtain a reasonable proficiency in the subject and a genuine awareness of some at least of the difficulties and pitfalls involved. You yourself Joe for a day or two last year suffered the misery of such an experience, did you not, when an idiot we all recall very well insisted in defiance of well-informed reliable advice based on years of hard-earned experience, that he would not endure the cost of a new drier and stubbornly refused to have one fitted with his replacement compressor, just because contrary to his expectation his insurance did not cover it - and we all remember pretty well what happened after that!

I was always a slow learner in some aspects of life, but two important truths have at least emerged at last for me. The first is that people may hammer away at my self-esteem as often and as long as they like, but while I have breath they can never destroy my spirit! The second is if they take away the tools of my trade and deny my God-given right to draw on the unique store of knowledge and experience which is mine alone I can no longer function effectively as a human being and the only logical conclusion that may be drawn from the standpoint of such a benighted analysis of my worth has to be that I might as well never have existed! I hope I am able to refute such an analysis now, which surely cries out against all sanity, sense, truth and justice! But while I acknowledge I am no saint myself, with faults and failings galore, I still wonder sometimes about the merits of life on a planet where so many takers and so many know-alls abound!

14.3.98

The furious conflict which regularly erupts between parents, with the father constantly and bitterly berating and belittling his fear-driven spouse that she offers him no affection and appears to have little or no motivation to please him or see to his needs (who can wonder after such treatment?), that the child's very survival seems constantly under threat. The pattern seems then to be set for the growing conviction that survival has to depend on the power of the unaided will alone, in self-sufficient isolation and without having any real ability to find or even acknowledge or become aware of the buried inner need to love and be loved by others, which may remain submerged and denied for many years in a desperate self-centred bid for fame or long-term financial security, the former to compensate for the deep sense of low self-worth which is such a burden to bear, the latter to somehow take care of the deep-rooted fear and insecurity which still pervades his life and lies at the heart of the problem.
Somehow such a person has to be freed from the fear, anger, guilt, distrust and self-loathing still seething within, which often arises in the victims of such an

upbringing. Above all he may need to feel loved and accepted for himself by another human being before ever he can have any real awareness of his own self-worth and value as a human being. (Dr Breggin, the eminent psychiatrist, appears to believe this is the only worthwhile approach in psychotic cases, as opposed to the application of drugs which relieve the pain but fail to solve the problem). The great difficulty with alcoholics, and some of their relatives, is the "letting go" of the relentless Juggernaut of self-will to a caring, loving power greater than themselves, (not necessarily God in the religious sense of the word), so that they can safely stop fighting everything and everybody and finally acknowledge and accept their own genuine weakness and vulnerability which is the true reality for every human being.

The spiritual sickness which is the most distressing symptom of my alcoholism is, I believe, due to my hopeless inability to love and care for those whom I know deep down I should, yet whom I treat so abominably, coupled with the meek, servile, people-pleasing image I present to my peers which I detest equally well, with no apparent ability to obtain any worthwhile, caring relationship with anyone, which I suspect everyone else seems capable of forming and maintaining except myself!

For the close relatives of alcoholics we usually recommend the support and assistance of Alanon or Alateen, sister fellowships to AA, but often there are not many takers at least until the alcoholic himself is fairly well on the road to recovery, which has taken me a lot of years because of the tranquillisers I was on, anti-psychotic drugs which I took for 25 years, initially to help withdraw from alcohol, but which persisted as a habit long after I picked up the bottle again.

Incredibly, with the help of all of AA,s twelve steps to recovery, which I had never properly been able to tackle before, being so divorced from my feelings by my medication, I managed at last to face the pain of my emotions, which although horrific at times, I have at last been able to do, along with the great help and on-going support of my friend and counsellor, Will, who regards so-called mental illness generally as more in the nature of a spiritual crisis or lack of balance, from which almost anyone can recover if they have the desire and are willing to try, however falteringly at first, the simple steps which he suggests.

Although I still have severe emotional difficulties at times, I would not have missed the life which has now opened up for me for anything in China! I still have to hand my self-will over to the guidance of my Higher Power and work the twelve steps of AA every single day, because alcoholism is an incurable, progressive illness even during recovery, but recovery nevertheless does bring undreamed-of rewards in terms of happiness and fulfilment to an extent I have never known before in my life, even though I could only hope to gain all of this from the final, desperate, and humbling admission of total powerlessness and defeat, both in respect to my alcohol obsession and ultimately, in the whole business of life itself.

For me the greatest truth which came out of all this, at least for me, who always considered himself so knowledgeable and clever for most of his life, despite having had such an obviously 'raw' deal right from the start, was the fundamental truth expressed in that well-known piece from the Bible,

"And though I have the gift of prophecy, and understand all mysteries, and all knowledge, and though I have all faith, so that I could remove mountains, and have not love, I am nothing."

29.3.98

Recalling the age-old story of the man who "fell among thieves" and by good fortune was helped by the good Samaritan, I wonder what the men of those days would think of today's "Samaritans" and all the other welfare workers and carers, private and government-financed support organisations who try to catch and comfort the endless flock of victims who fall prey every day to the thieves of loving comfort and security in our society as we know it today. Such are the mentally sick and disturbed, the nightmare victims of our fear-driven, self-seeking obsessive quest for personal achievement and success, which is obsessively inserted, as an overriding aim and necessity by parents, school-teachers and employers alike into the mind of every innocent child almost straight from the cradle with a ludicrous, insensitive, and often fanatical zest and enthusiasm.

One aspect of the story is written in the proudly glowing faces and the glowing school reports of those who achieve some measure of early success, so-called, together with the proud portrayal of places of honour in the charts and tables of success which our happy headmasters proudly present to their admiring colleagues, friends and families at every available opportunity.

The other, less happy side to the story is that of the gaunt, hollow-cheeked victims of such a barren, blinkered, and hopelessly inadequate set of values for living, who pace the corridors of our hospitals and treatment centres in their thousands, in their nightmare world of bewilderment and fear, where the horrific pain of living can often only be relieved by the application of powerful drugs, which may so reduce their capacity to feel and function happily as healthy human beings blessed with the gift of life, that any real hope of experiencing again the joy of living, which they knew briefly as children, has been stolen and taken from them.

Incredibly the only available criterion for their future happiness seems to be to return them somehow to the frantic rat-race world from which they were driven by its cruel misshapen view of the realities of life in the first place! Incredibly society sells us tragically short of our real potential for true happiness and fulfilment which is available to everyone if only we will listen to the voice of conscience, which is there as a guide for living in every one of us if only we will allow it to exist, and become aware of its immense significance as part of our God-given equipment for living.

Many regard mental illness generally as a spiritual sickness, where a sense of hopelessness and despair pervades the mind of the sufferer, instead of the healthy feelings of trust, faith, hope for the future, and genuine feelings of warmth and goodwill to others, upon which any chance of a happy and useful life must be based. The mentally sick or insane are surely nothing less than the product of an insanely self-centred, self-seeking populace, who while they lay claim to good principles and to a sound knowledge of right and wrong behaviour, in truth are so self-centred and self-seeking that their whole philosophy of living could well be summarised in the famous saying, "soul extinct, stomach well alive!", which originally was applied to the soldiers of an army on the move. How many in our society of today can honestly say they are not motivated and driven by the dog-eat-dog, devil-take-the-hindmost philosophy of living which permeates every office, shop, factory floor, boardroom and building where the leading priorities are output and efficiency, and nothing else really matters a damn. How many, I wonder, of our citizens can honestly say they are more concerned with giving than taking or acquiring what they can from life, of giving to their partner in terms of care, tolerance and understanding, rather than getting what they can for themselves from their relationship? How many employers can truthfully say they place a value on their employees as human beings who deserve good, just and honest treatment regardless of their use to the company as "cogs in the machine", and just how many company employees throughout the land can honestly say they feel they are more than just that, i.e. simply "cogs in a machine", and are genuinely willing to offer the best of themselves for the sake of the company and their employer?

What child at school who comes from a home where parental conflict perhaps has already begun to erode his security and confidence, is able to withstand with ease the demonic pressures and demands for achievement from his teachers, who may well turn from mentors into tormentors in the anxious mind of the child, who may frequently be assailed with worry and anxiety to "keep his teacher" happy and get his homework correct and "in on time", especially to avoid the misery of reprimand or punishment.

When this happens what should be for many a labour of love may well become a grim ordeal, where the real value and purpose of education is lost and subordinated to the frantic need to meet the insatiable demands of the teachers and the system, particularly in the attainment of arbitrary levels of performance in coursework and exams at particular stages and times, albeit the targets are tailored to match the varied abilities of each individual pupil. "Success" in such arbitrary aims is sometimes credited with such exaggerated importance that dire warnings couched in gruesome imagery on the penalties of failure are sometimes issued by teachers to parents anxious and eager to provide "the best" for their children and to guide and support them on the road to happy and useful lives. I wonder what some of the ancient Greeks, Plato maybe or Aristotle, might have thought of such an incredibly dramatised, myopic attitude to learning and the pursuit of knowledge. I wonder too what impact such pressures may have on the mind of the sensitive, frightened child who arrives at school straight from home, perhaps with the sound of parental strife and uproar still ringing in his ears, and with justified fear and anxiety tearing at his stomach.

The facts and the statistics surely speak for themselves. The coffins that carry our luckless suicides to their graves are as numerous now as those from death on our roads, as the sad succession continues of young lives brutally robbed of all hope, beaten, betrayed and broken, and sadly driven to self-destruct by the systemic lie that personal achievement and success are everything, and nothing else really matters in life. Even Shakespeare's Hamlet knew better than that, as he said to Horatio, "There are more things in heaven and earth than are dreamed of in your philosophy". Even the ancient Hebrews - and I have never been one for religion - knew better than that, when they wrote at the time of Moses, "When you reap the harvest of your land, do not reap to the very edges of your field or gather the gleanings of your harvest. Leave them for the poor..." The same message is repeated in another chapter, that "man does not live on bread alone", and the whole point and purpose of the Sabbath day of rest, as clearly stated in the commandment, was "so that your manservant and maidservant may rest, as you do."

Whoever gives themselves or anyone any rest these days, from the "liberated" working housewife overrun with household chores and worries for her children while at work as well as at home, the children themselves with their homework worries and concern to match as best they can the dreams and expectations of teachers and parents alike, while the unhappy father sweats with irreverent murmurings at the rebellious engine of his car on a Sunday morning, or worshipfully shines it instead, thinking of the day he can afford a better, more prestigious version of the same to match the one his fortunate neighbour owns, or maybe the one his wife would like but at present is way beyond the reach of his limited, stretched resources!

Meanwhile the misery of those who can find no rest in their minds or relief from the pain or fear of failure, continues to mount, with an estimated three million of our citizens being treated for depression alone at any one time, blindly seeking the same self-centred goals of personal success and accomplishment to which they were conditioned, yet which can never hope to bring the happiness, peace and fulfilment they richly deserve as human beings, if no attention is ever given to the need to care for and value the comfort, security and happiness of those with whom they share their lives. It is sad to reflect that lecturers, despite their training, knowledge and depth of understanding, like most of us are so dependent on the trappings of success which derive from the income of their job, that the moral and spiritual courage and resource to cope and find a way out of the abyss has not always been available to them when their job-security has been threatened, and many, as stated in Sinon Midgley's report in the TES of 27th March, "have retired through stress, depression or ill health" in recent years.

I cannot think that the price now being paid at every level in terms of human misery and shame throughout our society can possibly justify the continuing onslaught on the sanity and sensitivity of the minds of our young, many of whom now come from broken homes with divorce, separation and sexual infidelity commonplace everywhere, without at least some leavening of moral and spiritual training to help cope in some way with the misery of failure and rejection which everyone now and again encounters in life. Just a simple assurance from our teachers that we are all subject to failure at times, that no-one is exempt, would certainly help, coupled, dare I say it, if the courage is there, with the shocking and unpalatable, yet irrefutable truth, that success in exams is truly not the be-all and end-all of life, and that, thankfully, real success in terms of lasting happiness depends on far less demanding tasks, and actually arises far more readily from personal sacrifice and defeat, than from any accrual of knowledge, power or possessions.

I have found that sometimes failure in one major aspect of life, in spite of the pain of defeat, can sometimes lead to such success in a far more worthwhile endeavour, that nothing before could hope to match the abundant joy and satisfaction that such a success may bring, especially if the purpose and the motive is to give to others rather than to receive something back for oneself.

I can only pray that sometime, somehow, a measure of honesty, sanity and sense will return to a society which surely now has sadly lost its way and genuinely "got it wrong" in its fundamental philosophy and self-centred way of living.

(A victim and thief who spent many sad years in the wilderness.)

~

by Neville Lewis

Subsequent letters as new 'horizons' unfold

Anatomy of a Society

My Letter To Bob Dylan
14.6.98

Dear Mr Dylan,

You will probably not believe a word of this, but I feel I must tell you something of myself, if only for my own peace of mind.

I am a recovering alcoholic living in a small town in England. I am not writing for any purpose of gain, either for myself or the fellowship of Alcoholics Anonymous to which I belong, which in any case is not allowed to accept donations or gifts from any outside source. Nor would I wish for or welcome at all any publicity regarding what follows.

Nevertheless, I feel I should at least inform you that one of your recent CD compilations, of which I enclose the wrapper, appears in basic content to bear a remarkable resemblance to many of the events and circumstances relating to my own personal life over the past two years as I have withdrawn from medically prescribed tranquillisers which I have taken in one form or another since the age of 21 (I am now 58 years old), when I was first diagnosed as suffering from anxiety and depression.

Even the wapper appears to carry messages relevant to my current circumstances, especially with regard to my situation at work! I am bound to point out that no-one in the way of close family or friends seems willing to accept this assertion, nor even has bothered to listen to the CD in question, so I would not blame you in the least if you decide to "bin" this letter along with all the other 'lunatic' mail which presumably arrives now and then at the door of someone so famous.

But I hope you will read a little further, if only because I can identify with the awful "self-centredness" or preoccupation with self which, so at least I have read, you may yourself be afflicted, and which until very recently certainly characterised and blighted the greater part of my own life. The 'Big Book' of AA, as it is called, with which you may or may not be familiar, which was written in the 30's, identifies this self-centredness, on page 62, as being the root of the problem and the chief obstacle to recovery for any alcoholic, but I do believe now that this obsession with 'self' lies at the heart of many forms of emotional or so-called mental illness, and that the AA spiritual programme of recovery as outlined in the 12 steps in chapters 5 and 6 of the 'Big Book' may well hold the key to recovery for many such people who seem unable to be comfortable or at peace with themselves or anyone else for very long, unless under sedation of one form or another or when relief or comfort is obtained for a while, in some measure, from such things as the act of sex or any thrill such as gambling, all of which for many seems the only way of coping with the 'pain of living', for which they regularly, as I did myself for many years, blame others, or their environment, or their ill fortune in life, or countless other circumstances or factors outside their own control.

For at least 10 years in the fellowship of AA I only managed to cope without alcohol because I was still taking tranquillisers. When I finally admitted to myself that my life really was "unmanageable", as I should have done from the start, and that I must stop 'playing God' and trying so hard to control my own and other people's lives, I began at last to hand over my self-will and my entire life to a "power greater than myself" or God as I understand Him on a daily basis, which is in effect the 3rd step of the AA programme and forms the only valid or viable basis for lasting recovery for most alcoholics, leading to the "house cleaning" steps and ultimately the removal of the awful feelings of isolation, distrust and often despair which characterise so many forms of mental (or 'spiritual') illness. Only when I found the courage at last to surrender my will and my life to God every single day was I able to stop my tablets for good, and that has to be a blessing of great magnitude for someone so sedated that I could barely feel or enjoy or appreciate anything of beauty for many years except through a kind of fog that got in the way of everything worthwhile in life.

It says in the Big Book that "when we sincerely took such a position, remarkable things followed", and I can certainly testify to that, as I will shortly explain. But the greatest discovery for me was to become aware of my total failure in life to feel anything like "genuine" love or affection for others without expectation of return or reward, and with no nagging fear or misgiving that my trust might be misplaced and that the recipient of my affection might one day desert me at some point in the future if the opportunity arose. In the end I found the real 'me' is after all the happy, fun-loving, caring and trusting little chap which is surely God's intention for us all in the first place - until society, via parents and schooling, prints its own programme of fears and restraints on to the innocent mind of the child, and manages to change many or most of us into mis-shapen monsters or machines, sometimes so centred on self and our self-centred cravings that very little room is left for genuine love or respect, either for ourselves or anyone else.

The process of "cleaning house", as we call it in AA, whereby all the dreadful fears and resentments from our past, often obscured or denied by stubborn layers of false pride or self-justification, are eventually identified and removed, can be an extremely painful and humbling process indeed. I did great harm behind closed doors in frustration and anger, and not only when drinking, to all of my family, the worst victim being my own first son, who actually gave me your amazing CD for Xmas (!), whom I beat and maltreated horribly as a boy, and who has only recently returned home from the local hospital heavily drugged and sedated, and who I pray to God one day will make a full and happy recovery.

Yet in spite of the foregoing, the horror and shame of which I shall never forget, I truthfully do not believe myself to be the worthless monster which such a picture paints, and which for years kept me a prisoner fearful of, exposure and leading the "double life" of a 'Jekyll and Hyde' so common with alcoholics and many others whose lives are distorted and driven by fear, anger and guilt. To discover, as I have, that I am truthfully not a 'bad' person, but that deep down I do in fact care a great deal for others after all, has come as an enormous relief to me as well as a source of great strength and hope for the future., even though I know it must be a long time before I can expect to be fully forgiven by my family, if indeed that will ever be possible in my own lifetime. If they manage to find a real measure of peace and happiness, which at last is coming to me, that will more than suffice and would constitute the greatest gift I could wish to receive in my remaining years.

To have discovered this simple truth, albeit "so far on" in my life, as track 16 says, is something I shall always cherish as the greatest blessing I have ever received from the God of my understanding. Although I will never be perfect, at least I know that it was never my own real wish or intention that any such harm as I did to others should come from my own sick hand, or indeed from my vicious, venomous tongue which I hope has finally learned its lesson and ceased its hurt or blame of others. At least there is consolation too in knowing it is an illness and that, as it says in the Big Book, "many of us had moral and philosophical convictions galore, but we could not live up to them even though we would have liked to. Neither could we reduce our self-centredness much by wishing or trying on our own power. We had to have God's help." Ultimately it is only by finding, seeing and "embracing" again the innocent child of my early life that I have been able to see any trace of the goodness in me which somehow survived the misery and all the denial, first of my spiritual sickness which I found was 'inside me' after all, then ultimately of my own underlying decency and goodness which surely is innate in every human being, however damaged or disturbed by the foolish fears and delusions induced by the self-centred, self-seeking aims of a society which sadly has got its priorities wrong! How well I remember my first psychiatrist, at a time when I was still overwhelmed with fear and anxiety after several months' treatment, adding fuel to the flames by saying I should not cancel my college course as yet, for that would be "burning my boats". Perhaps she thought I lived on a desert island, or maybe that I needed to be a Plato or an Aristotle to come back from this one successfully at such a critical time of life! In hindsight the only crucial truth concerning time for me has been that the whole idea is a myth and a ploy where learning and education are concerned, and I doubt whether Plato or Aristotle would have taken too kindly to the broiler chicken approach, assuming they had sufficient strength and stamina to stay the course in the hot-house conditions of the "system" as we know it today!

I must acknowledge that the CD has helped to keep my hopes alive as I have suffered the pains of "waking up" to reality: I was sure the answers would come sooner or later when I heard the words, "I see my life come shining from the west down to the east; any day now, any day now I shall be released!" For that is precisely the journey I believe I had to take, from the present day right back to my earliest memory, when I was a child in my mother's arms as she crouched under the kitchen table during an air raid early on in the war, as German bombers passed directly overhead many times on their way to the capital. I have felt a great deal of fear at times and have prayed again and again for God to remove it along with all my other defects, as per step 7 of the AA programme, and I believe that most of it now has at last been taken away, for I feel so happy at times I have even found myself singing, just like I did as a boy! It has been a great joy also to learn that the truth, when we do go back far enough in our lives, doesn't hurt at all, because the simple truth is that God really does love all of His creation and longs for us to love him back the same as any earthly father would! I am convinced that no child was ever born inherently bad or evil, nor indeed that such emotive words are even relevant to anything. It is just that most of us are given the wrong advice or worse in the way of neglect or unfair treatment by parents or mentors who themselves were trained and educated to follow the wrong principles in fear and anxiety for most of their own lives, in a society where committed love and respect for the truth, the most vital and necessary ingredients for the growth of trust and security in the mind of any child, so often are sadly offered at a price or only on condition other goals are successfully met. The moment we apply a price or condition to love the innocent logic of any child must surely assume that failure to meet the condition must mean that some of the love may be withdrawn. Although most parents would be loathe to admit it, is this not precisely what many or most of us do in our anxiety to ensure that our luckless children "succeed" , when we insist they finish their homework, or stay in as a punishment for not completing it the day before, or urge them to put in extra effort because the teacher says they "could do better" - when perhaps they feel they are doing the best they can anyway? Any pressure or superimposed condition, of which there are so many for most of us in life, which threatens to restrict or prevent the flow of love on which the child depends is liable also to inhibit its own freedom to express love and thereby damage the natural trust and spontaneity which is so essential to the formation of caring, loving relationships as the child's personality unfolds and blossoms into maturity in later life. How many parents can say they are truthfully unconcerned about their children getting enough grades to secure the 'right job' or having 'enough money' coming in to 'run their own home' before they think of getting married or 'starting a family', or are not constantly at pains to ensure their children are responsible and willing to do whatever is expected of them without complaint! How many are concerned instead to ensure above all else that their children are free as much as possible from fear and worry and that they know that nothing can ever separate them from the flow of their parents' love! There is nothing wrong with being successful at anything, or with making or having money, or having a palatial home or a prosperous business or anything at all, as long as committed love comes first before any other aims or considerations. That was the simple message which was passed to us as long ago as Moses and repeated by Christ in the New Testament, that love must come first, love of God who gave us life and all that we have in the first place, then love for our neighbours as much as for ourselves - in other words committed or "true love" in the fullest meaning of the word, where nothing matters more than the welfare and happiness of the one who is loved. The need for truth and honesty in all our dealings with one another is also clearly and emphatically stated in the books of Deuteronomy and Leviticus in the Old Testament, which are also mentioned on the "Sugarman" track. To be sure, come what may, of the love of one's parents, to be convinced that others in society really do care about us and are ready to offer more than just tea and sympathy in time of need, and to know that everyone prefers to be honest - even in today's world there are very few who relish being caught out in a lie, yet fewer still who are not tempted at times to lie for gain - with such a foundation for life there surely would be few children born without a real chance for lasting happiness and fulfilment in every possible way. At present Esther Ranson's childline receives more than 10, 000 calls every single day, of which only around 3000 can be answered because of insufficient volunteers. I have read that more than 3 million people in Britain are receiving treatment for depression alone at any given time, and that suicides in our society are now as numerous as deaths on the roads. While on holiday recently I was reminded in various places that I could take care of my child's future welfare with a simple £10 starter investment, as though money can be the cure-all or solution to everything, while in numerous phone boxes I was greeted by the pleasing, smiling face of a well-formed female or male with the well-intentioned but fatuous caption that "The best things in life are free" ... in my experience that has to be the most arrant nonsense and denial of the truth I have ever seen - and yet it should and could become the reality and truth for most of us if only children were given proper priority treatment from the start and society managed to get its priorities right!

by Neville Lewis

Meanwhile for many the notion of 'true love' is about as remote and unreal as the idea of Heaven itself or even the existence of God or any Creator or "power greater than" our own ego, intellect or personal will.

For myself I must admit I have come to think very differently over the course of the last two years, and more so than ever during the last few weeks, when my life has become decidedly hectic! For one thing I have been woken in the middle of the night by the deep-throated roar of a wild-cat in woods where I was 'sleeping out' and forced to flee terror-stricken to a nearby hotel where 'fortuitously', I was later informed, a late-night guest had left the hotel by a side-door which no-one had bothered to lock! I must admit I felt so sure the reference on the CD, "a wild-cat did growl", must refer to one of the women of my acquaintance - perhaps indeed my wife! - which just goes to show how miserably wrong one can be! I've spent a fortnight away on my own for the first time ever, and the very first day I was whisked by taxi to Glasgow Western Infirmary, thinking I was about to collapse with another heart attack, only to be informed there was nothing whatever wrong with me and what on earth was I doing there anyway? Whereupon I really went crazy and threw away all my heart tablets which I had been told 6 years earlier I would have to take for the rest of my life, and promptly went on to climb three sizeable mountains, including the highest in the land, where I spent the night exhausted on the summit in a 'bothie' or hut which had the word 'Dylan' scrawled in huge lettering across one of the inside walls. By this time I am thinking there surely must be some cure for this sort of thing, and any more of this 'shit' and I'd rather be dead anyway! I cannot say either that I would normally choose to wander unwittingly late at night through one of the worst areas of Glasgow, especially with my nervous disposition, where I was solicited by young men in cars, and later offered sex by three sad young girls on a building site, who all claimed to be motherless, one of whom was clearly distressed. Then as I talked briefly to them I was promptly warned by a youth to clear off because the man(?) looking after them was getting 'restless'! No doubt this was the "Sodom and Gomorrah" of the Sugarman track where "no-one would want to marry your sister". I never had a sister, only brothers. That was quite a night to remember, because for good measure every time I felt like stopping to find somewhere to stay for the night a voice seemed to keep saying, "remember what you did to your son", and somehow I knew I had to keep walking for his sake! I cried quite a bit that night, and it was dawn before I was able to stop and get a little broken sleep in my "bivvy" on a piece of grass behind some houses. (This was all prior to my mountain-climbing madness!)

Finally, after miscellaneous other strenuous and unexpected adventures, on my return to work I again found myself bombarding my poor lady-friend in the office with yet more poetry and protestations of undying love - the "nightingale tune" of the CD of course, endeavouring somehow, as ever, to keep "one step ahead of the prosecutor within" because she and I both happen to be married with children, for Christ's sake!

Alcoholics are notoriously prone to obsessions, but this one appears, despite every prayer and supplication, to be totally solid and immoveable, so it looks as if I shall be bearing the cross of unrequited love, on top of everything else, on my shoulders for the rest of my days! As luck has it, despite being a truly warm and loveable person, she was forced in her desperate search for love and happiness, to abandon two very young children, under pressure to return to a husband she was unable to love, one of whom still refuses, some years on, to allow any contact with her in spite of her pleas. Meanwhile I am living away from home in a £300 caravan to try to simmer down and settle my scattered wits as best I can, having come to the reluctant conclusion that my wife of many years doesn't really care about my emotional needs at all and truthfully never has. I have also finally packed in my job after moaning about it for years, and on hearing the news my elder son suggested, quite rightly, that Mum bake a cake!

I suppose in statute law there must somewhere be provision for this kind of behaviour. I just hope no news of it leaks out and reaches the wrong ears, in case they consider reviving the old feudal law and deal with me as they did with poor Simon de Montfort, who is said to have founded our parliament, by having me "hanged, drawn and quartered", and my remains "thrown to the dogs!" As long as it was deemed 'politically correct,' I guess it wouldn't matter much anyway!

ANON

~

David Ruffley (MP) - House of Commons
13.7.98

As you will see from the enclosed I am trying my best to draw attention to my current plight in Bury St Edmunds. I have managed to obtain the promise of an initial payment of around £48.00 into my bank in Sudbury by way of income support, to be credited to my account on Wednesday of this week, which I have requested be set aside for my personal use for the time being (rather than repay any outstanding indebtedness at this point in time) which I believe they will go along with.

I would like very much to stay for a while in Scotland, with a strong inclination to remain there on a permanent basis at some point in the future, without having to commit myself to such a move until I am more relaxed and secure in the knowledge that my basic needs for sustenance and shelter are firmly in place before I rush off again without thinking!

The dilemma facing me at present, which seems so silly, is simply how my particular needs at this time can be defined or categorised so as to comply with all the regulations appropriate to my situation both in Scotland and England without jeopardising or restricting my own simple requirements and those of my family here in England. I would very much like to stay in youth hostels for a while, mainly in the Highland areas of Scotland, where I can freely mix with others who enjoy the scenery and the walking much as I do, and I can really be free from the hassles and pressures I have been under for so long both at home and in the workplace, at least for a while.

Unfortunately, however, it appears I would be classified as a "holidaymaker" by the Stirling Council, in such a scenario, which would only attract about £20.00 a week in terms of housing benefit, which truthfully would be cutting things a bit fine, whereas I would be entitled to full benefit in a convalescent home, which with regret, I consider wholly inappropriate to my present need. A fixed address might, again, attract full benefit, but only by making a firm commitment in writing of my intention to take up permanent residence in Scotland. But the most alarming, and disconcerting consideration which I now understand may apply and which effectively for me would disqualify the whole idea, was the suggestion from an official at the DSS in Stirling that I would not be eligible for ongoing income support because of the existing equity in my home here in England which I would (presumably) first have to obtain and exhaust to a degree, before returning for ongoing income support should it still be necessary after my current sick note from Dr Harcourt in Bury St Edmunds, expires. This I will not do in any event, as it would mean selling my house, where my wife and children would prefer to remain. Other means of obtaining access to any of my share of the equity (Roughly £20.000) without physically selling up appear, in my present circumstances, unavailable or at best very remote.

If you or anyone could somehow arrange for a category to be opened or defined by legitimate means, without unfair preference or favour to me in any way as an individual, to suit if possible, my particular needs as outlined above, I would be grateful indeed, but if your hands are also tied I will accept the situation with equanimity as best I can and have another "think" as to where I can happily "disappear" for a while, perhaps somewhere in England such as the Yorkshire Dales, assuming such a scheme is acceptable to the appropriate authorities in this country without jeopardising my needs or those of my family.

Thank you for your interest in this matter,

(This, of course, was written after I ran out of money and became homeless while in Scotland, struggling to recover from my failed love for Shirley, who remained loyal and true to her husband, and an extremely stressful marriage. It was written while staying briefly in the marital home. After being warned I could not stay for long, as my wife herself was now living on state support and my continued presence could jeopardise her right to state benefit, I scrounged ten pounds from my poor wife and in desperation hiked and hitched my way back to Scotland.)

Share Magazine
18.05.06

I was a 'dry', two-stepping fraud in AA for twelve miserable years, with one face for my luckless family and another face to the outside world. When at last I reached a second rock-bottom without the drink, I finally did all the steps of the programme, exactly as per the Big Book, and found a measure of peace I had never known before.
I'm not much of a poet, but I thought you might like to include the following poem, entitled 'The Love Within', in your magazine, which describes the wonderful spiritual change which took place in my life after many grim years in 'the wilderness.'

'The Love Within'

I wanted to love
But I hated instead,
I outwardly smiled
But inwardly bled,

For hating denies
The yearning within
To love and be loved by

by Neville Lewis

Our own kith and kin.

Yet hard as I tried
To love as I should,
The anger inside
All my efforts withstood,

Until I came
To a wall so sheer,
Built in shame
With anger and fear,

That at last I was forced
To face the pain
And beg on my knees
For help once again.

And from that moment on
A song was begun,
Which was there in my heart -
As in everyone.

At first just a murmur
Hardly heard,
It now fills my being
With every word,

And every word
Says love is divine,
A gift from God
That can even be mine!

And beauty, truth and joy now abound
Where once only hatred and fear could be found...

~

Helen Yates
Public Communications Unit
Department for Education and Skills
24-11-06

Thank you for your letter of 22nd November 2006, in reply to mine on the subject of fear of failure and how it affects children in schools.

It is one thing to make all sorts of lovely rules to govern the way teachers teach - it is another to make sure such rules are observed by every teacher across the board, so that the health and well-being of every child is protected and guaranteed.

Furthermore, how can you possibly be certain that "tests are administered in a manner which causes minimal anxiety to the children," when it is simply not possible to measure anxiety - until it's too late and the damage is done.

You clearly must live on another planet!

by Neville Lewis

Kierran Horner
Customer Service Centre
Dept of Health
18-09-06

Thank you for your letter of 8th September 2006, in which you state that "between 2001/02 and 2005/6, NHS and local authority planned expenditure on mental health services has increased in real terms by 25%." This comes as no surprise, given the number of broken relationships and households in turmoil these days, as well as the hectic pace and extreme pressures of modern-day living.

With respect, I suggest it would make better sense to reduce the pressures upon our young, by making homework optional and replacing the stress of formal exams, on which so much is made to depend, with teacher-assessments instead. Surely no child or young person should ever be deemed to have 'failed' where learning is concerned, which is a 'non-sense' in itself! In my case, my self-esteem sank to an all-time low when I failed to gain a degree, bearing in mind all the hype which surrounds 'success' and the high expectations of all my teachers. From then on I saw myself as 'a failure' in life, a feeling and a belief which was incredibly hard to remove and which fuelled an increasing addiction to alcohol.

In recent years I have come to believe that our children's health would greatly improve if they were encouraged to learn in a spirit of mutual support and co-operation, rather than fierce competition, which must leave many 'poor performers' with a diminished sense of self-worth. For the same reason, it would surely make sense to provide the option of an earlier leaving age for those who are happy to join the 40% of our workforce who are engaged in unskilled, repetitive tasks for the provision of vital goods and services - without whom we would not survive. In truth, I see no 'better' or more important job than that of a factory worker on a production line, a refuse collector, storeman or humble shop-assistant - however much we applaud or reward the accomplishments of our expanding intelligentsia. As for odious 'league tables', I see no point in struggling for ever, at great effort and cost, to bring all our schools into line, as good teachers and scholars are born, not made, while social factors affecting performance will always vary from school to school and region to region.

I submit that happy children grow into happy, healthy adults, and if we made the changes I have suggested, I am convinced we would see far fewer cases of mental ill health, addiction or crime in years to come, with huge potential savings in health care and law-enforcement costs. Meanwhile, with more choices and more time for children to socialise after school, perhaps many more would take up the love which comes to us all in our teens, the most precious gift we can have, despite the perverse disregard for the value of pubic love which our culture appears to maintain.

To David Ruffley MP
Shadow Minister for Welfare Reform
8-11-06

Thank you for the letter from Jim Knight, the Minister of State for Schools and 14-19 Learners, who states that "homework is not compulsory," which must be a huge relief for many school-children, especially those who come from broken or disturbed homes - bearing in mind that one in six families are believed to be plagued by domestic violence.

I enclose the latest statistics on mental illness in children aged 5 to 16, which clearly show how important happy, lasting parental relationships are for the health and well-being of all our young, while any reduction in pressure on children must help a great deal. Life is uncertain and makes many demands at the best of times, and I have long believed that excessive, unreasonable pressure, both in schools and the workplace, is the main cause of mental and physical illness in our society today, which is why constant testing, inspections and league tables, which put so much pressure on teachers and children alike, in my view should be abandoned. The instinct to learn is natural to all human beings, and I submit that most people give of their best in whatever they do, when they are given the right motivation - without being pushed or coerced. (To the best of my knowledge, the Ancient Greeks, who taught us so much, had no pressure upon them at all.) For that reason, I do applaud the decision to provide employer designed specialised courses for 14 to 19-year olds, as most of the knowledge we sweat to obtain for the sake of exams, unless it interests us, is soon lost to memory through lack of use, so a great deal of time and effort is wasted.

The misguided "drive for higher standards" in schools based on intense government pressure exacts a heavy price. By my reckoning, 10% of all children having "a clinically recognised mental illness" equates to more than a million individuals, which must place great strain (and cost) on our mental health services. It also amounts to an appalling measure of suffering inflicted on innocent children by our free and caring (?) society.

(Although schools are given the option, in practice, of course, very few children are free from the burden of compulsory homework!)

by Neville Lewis

The Times
27-11-06

In schools, the word 'success' is often used in an absolute sense to extract maximum effort from pupils, with the clear implication that there is no worthwhile future for those who 'fail'. So sensitive, innocent children must therefore view 'failure' as utterly unthinkable. I may be stupid, but I don't understand how any child can be deemed to have 'failed' where learning is concerned.

Knowledge is power, but love, both for ourselves and others around us, is surely much more important - although when I asked an A-level teacher what comfort there is for students who fail their exams, or don't get the grades that they need, the lady, sadly, was absolutely dumbfounded.

Yours is a newspaper steeped in tradition, but I hope you acknowledge the need for change to our increasingly pressurised system of education - bearing in mind that one in ten children aged 5 to 16 have "a clinically recognised mental disorder", while every day ten people in their twenties take their own lives. That's a heavy price to pay for optimum 'performance' in schools - especially when most of the knowledge we gain, unless it attracts our interest, is soon lost to memory through lack of use!

Woraphan Lagkam
Customer Service Centre
Department of Health
12-1-07

Thank you for your letter of 8-1-2007.

I have to say that I am more interested in the prevention of serious illness than its diagnosis and treatment, and I am convinced that addiction and mental illness especially, usually arise from a 'lack of love' during early life.

When I was a boy, coitus was viewed as the natural consummation of love, rather than some kind of pastime or sensual experience which one indulged in 'for kicks'. and which as you know is now widely displayed and glorified in films and sit-coms in people's homes throughout the land.

I am convinced that we need to start talking about love, especially the love which comes to us all around the time of puberty, when we are under such pressure in school to 'do well' that there doesn't seem time to focus on love and to see it succeed. When later we try to choose for ourselves on the basis of superficial attraction the outcome, as we all know, is often disastrous.

I suggest it is the failure of early love, combined with the pressures of schooling, which more than anything else sets the scene for promiscuous sex and all kinds of other unhealthy obsessions, including addiction to drink or drugs and under- or over-eating, as we search for consolation from the pain of failed love and the pressures of everyday living.

I should know. I've been there myself.

The Bury Free Press
4-11-06

I understand, from reliable sources, that some NHS carers in Bury, who give a vital service to elderly people living alone, are only allowed fifteen minutes per visit, including travelling time, sometimes to outlying villages, so they are forced to work well into the evening to cover all their calls. I understand also that some fully-trained nurses are having to spend half their valuable time dealing with mounting paperwork - at the insistence of their managers. Meanwhile, it has been widely reported that staff in our hospitals are forced to resort to tricks and stratagems to manipulate waiting times, in order to meet their targets, which have become a major distraction from patient care and an extra burden to bear.

I suggest, if most of the faceless, time-wasting bureaucrats, who now run, or rather ruin, our health service, were given the sack, if paperwork was cut to a minimum and odious 'targets' abolished, there would be more money available to maintain staffing levels and more motivation for those at the sharp end who do the caring - i.e. our dedicated doctors, nurses and support workers, whose sole aim has always been to alleviate human suffering in every way that they can.

The Department of Work and Pensions
6-12-06

Whenever I ring my local B & Q store in Bury St Edmunds, just seeking advice on a product, their phone rings and rings, with no-one, it seems, available to answer my call. It does seem that some companies (and institutions), which have a near-monopoly on the service they give - including the Post Office and the Department of Work and Pensions, as well as others, are grossly under-manned.

by Neville Lewis

At a time when unemployment nationwide has risen to one and a half million, while many employees are stretched to the limit of their capacity - in some cases making them ill - it scarcely makes sense to keep so many willing workers idle on the dole, receiving state support, some of whom may resort to crime or benefit abuse to help make ends meet.

If our government insisted that such companies (and institutions) took on more staff, there would be fewer people on the dole receiving state support and less pressure on those in the workplace, while waiting times for essential services to the public at large would greatly be reduced - at no extra cost to the community as a whole.

Sadly, private companies tend to think only of profit, while most politicians are cursed with myopic vision.

Bury Free Press
6-03-07

I was concerned to hear that our Government intends to turn to the private sector to persuade the long-term unemployed and some of our sick to get back into work. Private companies are mainly concerned to make as much profit as they can for the owners, so they are unlikely to show much compassion for those who are mentally sick and who may not be able to cope with the pressures involved in most places of work, bearing in mind that no job these days is secure.

National statistics reveal that financial security is vital to the health and well-being of every human being. For example, the richer we are, the more likely we are to live longer than fifty, while the incidence of lung cancer is much higher than the national average in deprived areas, such as Manchester, Liverpool and Glasgow. I am therefore convinced we will see more and more mentally sick people relapsing and requiring hospital treatment, at great cost to the NHS, if the planned changes go through. Meanwhile, the proposed reduction in financial support for single Mums will surely lead to more latch-key children and therefore more anti-social behaviour in years to come.

Contrary to popular belief, people are not naturally lazy, but they do need to feel secure.

Anatomy of a Society

The Times
19-01-07

It's all very well to talk about being 'racist' towards our coloured countrymen in the UK or elsewhere. The convenience store near my home is run by a Moslem from Bangladesh. However nice and polite I may be in my dealings with him, as he is with me, how can I know for sure he won't blow me and my neighbours apart if I happen to say 'the wrong thing'?

ANON

The Bury Free Press
6-5-07

Can it be wise to use phrases like "sink or swim", "success or disaster", and "academic suicide", all of which were used at an information session for parents at one of our schools?

Happy children, free from anxiety and fear, make much better scholars, so I see no sense in such an approach to learning. The instinct to learn is natural to all human beings from the day we are born, and fear of failure can reap a terrible harvest of misery and pain, especially for children from broken or disturbed homes. For the same reason, I see no merit in stressful exams or compulsory homework, nor in the cruel blackmail that children have "only one chance to succeed."

Learning should be a labour of love, and I submit that the culture of 'winners and losers' should be abandoned in favour of teachers' reports and recommendations, after close consultation with each individual pupil. Surely all of our young should be treated as 'winners', given the fact that they all have to spend most of their childhood engaged in the learning process! Too much pressure can have disastrous results, as witness the fact that an horrific one in ten children aged five to sixteen have "a clinically recognised mental disorder."

We all have a value as human beings, and at the end of the day real 'success' depends on how well we enjoy the work that we do and how well it suits our particular talents, both in school and the workplace, whether our fate is to work on a production line in a factory or to achieve fame as an eminent scientist, poet or politician.

by Neville Lewis

Dr Athar Yawar
The Lancet
30-05-07

Thank you so much for your kind letter of 25th May 2007. I enclose a couple of extracts from a small book that I wrote five years ago, entitled 'The Truth About Love', which I regret has never been published. The piece about anger and resentments was written at least ten years ago, around the time I fell hopelessly in love with a married woman at work and withdrew from a very unhappy and stressful relationship, which had groaned on for twenty-five years!

During my time in hospital, it seemed to me that most of my fellow patients were consumed with anger and fear, which frequently came from a 'lack of love' at some point in their past, which they couldn't forgive, or else from a recent traumatic event in their lives, which left them isolated and thereby unable to cope.

Counselling and support is often given to people affected by traumatic events, such as the London bombings, yet it seemed to me that the hospital psychiatrists were only interested in treating the symptoms of those in their care, instead of the reasons behind their distress - in my case the fact I'd been homeless for four months in a desperate search for affordable accommodation before I became ill.

With regard to the drug Stelazine, a friend recommended it to me to help me withdraw from alcohol, but sadly I quickly became addicted, and after twenty-five years on the drug, it was only with help from sustained counselling, and support from the woman at work, that I was able to get through the truly 'horrific' withdrawals. Nonetheless, I did have two really good years free from pills, until unexpectedly, I found myself homeless.

At least I've been able to discharge most of my recent anger regarding my 'treatment' in writing, while relations with my former partner and two fine sons have greatly improved since we separated. I have also discharged all my debts, despite my low income, so I do have a measure of peace I have never known before - and that in spite of my ongoing 'medication'.

Dr Athar Yawar
The Lancet
26-01-08

Dear Athar Yawar,

I hardly know how to thank you for your letters, which have sustained me during a difficult time in my life. The best I can do is to send you a copy of my letter to the famous singer, Bob Dylan, which I wrote ten years ago and which I handed in to the theatre in Glasgow where he was performing, hoping he might get to read it. The CD in question was given to me by my son Mathew as a Christmas present - a most wonderful gift from the son I had treated so badly when he was a child. I am so happy that he has forgiven the past and that we now are the best of friends.

I know how sceptical you must be about my perceived 'links' with a piece of music which was composed long ago, especially as I've been mentally ill, but I can assure you that I was perfectly sane at the time. The CD itself begins with the words, "How many roads must a man walk down, before yer call him a man?" and ends with the words, "Beauty walks on a razor's edge - someday I'll make it mine!" I don't even know if it is still available in the shops, but I do know it had a huge impact on me when I first heard it, along with a CD by Paul Robeson, which began with the words, "Look down, look down that lonesome road before you travel on..."

It certainly has been 'a lonesome road' at times, but your letters have made the going easier and I do thank you for that. I wouldn't expect you as a psychiatrist to give any credence at all to any claim by a person to have made 'conscious contact' with God, in spite of the fact it is mentioned as part of the eleventh step of the programme of Alcoholics Anonymous!

God bless you!

Andrew Phillips
21-03-08

Thank you so much for your kind letter. I was delighted to hear from you.

I am quite philosophical about my past, but I can't seem to stop writing letters to prominent members of the establishment, based on my own life experience and what I perceive to be truth. A friend calls me a philosopher-activist, but others (including Baroness Williams) may well think of me as a pain in the neck!

by Neville Lewis

My greatest mistake (?) was to fall hopelessly in love with a married woman at work when I was 56 - after having been married for 25 years to a sweet lady, Mary, who gave us two very fine sons, Mathew and Mark.

Falling in love at such a late age turned my life upside down. I separated from my poor wife, hoping my 'true love' would join me, but she remained loyal and true to her husband and family. For a while, I even was homeless, tramping the streets for several months with no money to pay for accommodation. (I am much more prudent with money now!) But all that was ten years ago. I now have a comfortable flat which I rent very cheaply from Havebury Housing Partnership. I see my family nearly every day and although we are now merely friends, my wife and I are much happier since we separated. I am also lucky indeed to have plenty of time to write and to go on long walks in the countryside, which I love.

Thanks again for your letter, which I reckon my family will frame!

P.S. My parents weren't 'bad' parents at all. It's just that my poor father was badly affected by the War, as I learned later after he died.

Patricia Hewitt
Sec of State for Health
1.09.06

The other day I was walking a long-distance path, when I encountered a herd of cows with their calves, close by the route I needed to take. I knew that cows can be dangerous when they are with their young, so with my heart in my mouth and gasping for breath, I somehow skirted around them and made it safely to the stile at the end of the field. I have noticed that whenever I suffer from fear, anxiety or anger, the stress affects my breathing and no doubt my heart rate as well.

I am still convinced that emotional stress plays a much bigger role than we think in the general causation of illness. I have noticed that women have much more emotional strength than most men, which may explain why females tend to live longer than males and get better results than boys in exams - except perhaps for the more demanding sciences. A recent survey has shown that rich people are more likely to live beyond the age of 50 than those who are forced to cope with the worry of being poor and financially insecure. Studies have also revealed that the blood-pressure of breast-fed babies, with their Mums in attendance all day, is one point lower on average than that of babies fed with a bottle. I understand also that the incidence of asthma is very high in young children in the UK, where mothers are given incentives to go out to work and to leave their children with carers. I submit that 'care' is a poor substitute for a mother's love, although many mothers are obliged to work just to make ends meet. Only 2% of children raised in care go on to higher education, while studies have shown that people who receive hugs from family and friends, i.e. are loved from the start, are less likely to suffer a heart attack in later life.

My friends have all suffered some form of mental ill health. One lost his Mum when he was ten months old and was raised by his Dad and his step-sister, who constantly argued and fought with each other. As an adult he admits he was an obsessive womaniser and violent alcoholic, who constantly got into fights. He had a serious heart attack when still quite young and assures me the only real love he ever received in his life is the love he gets from his cats. Another friend had a violent mother who battered her husband and turned her own daughter out on the street. (He has managed to kick the drug problem he had, but has been kept for some years under section, for fear he might harm himself with his anger.) Another friend, who became an alcoholic, was running from home at the age of six and had to stand up in court at the age of eight to choose between his Mum and his Dad. Another friend became ill when he discovered he wasn't the father of one of his children. I also once met a hopeless alcoholic, whose wife confided that his troubles had all begun when he learned, at the age of nineteen, that he had been abandoned as a baby by his real Mum. His wife also admitted he regularly beats her and that she no longer shares his bed, because he consorts with prostitutes. He also has a serious heart condition. A woman I knew while in hospital, who also was mentally ill and could no longer be trusted to care for her children, appears to have fallen ill for the same reason, i.e. she too learned she had been abandoned by her true mother when very young. I also met a woman I knew from my childhood, who said she was trying to get over a drink problem, and happened to mention she lost her mother when she was only eight years old.

In my case, my mother was unfaithful in the marital bed with a soldier during the war, an act which my father never forgave, so there was constant conflict between my parents throughout my childhood and youth. I can remember how lonely and angry I felt as a boy and how fear gripped my stomach whenever I thought that my mother might leave to escape my father's wrath. At school I was the teachers' pet, but my performance fell off as I became more and more depressed and I suffered a serious mental breakdown at the age of 21, which put paid to my university career. As I grew older I turned more and more to drink for consolation and relief from the anger within, and brought grief and suffering to my poor wife and family for many grim years. Later, a counsellor ascribed my own heart attack to suppressed anger inside, rather than smoking, because his school of counselling has discovered a link between suppressed anger and heart disease.

Of course, bingeing on food is another way of coping with stress, which may well explain the growing problem of obesity in children, with its harmful impact on health.

When we receive love, we give out love and remain in good health, but anger and fear make us ill. Where are the happy relationships and where is the love in our loveless society today? Last year there were 186,000 abortions in the UK, which doesn't say much for the judgement, modesty or self-control of the ladies concerned, although they too, no doubt, were probably starved of love in early life.. I wonder how many foolish acts of infidelity go unrecorded, and how any self-respecting young man can hope to find love with a hardened whore.

True love propitiously comes to us all around the time of puberty, and we can all recall the name of the loved one the rest of our lives. I submit that such love would last a lifetime if given the chance, but seldom succeeds as its value is widely denied by parents and teachers alike. They and our politicians are more interested to see how our children 'perform' under pressure, all through their childhood and youth.

If we wish for a happy, healthy and peaceful society, I suggest we respect the emotional needs of our young by reducing the pressure upon them and giving them all the love that we can.

Marjorie Wallace
'SANE'
16-10-06

Thank you very much for your letter in response to my correspondence to Patricia Hewitt, which I copied to 'SANE'.

I'm afraid there is some doubt as to whether the Secretary of State got to read my letters, as the response came from the 'Customer Service Centre', and as you can see from the two letters enclosed, the issues I raised were never addressed or even mentioned.

While I applaud any effort to treat mental illness when it occurs, I still think society needs to change in a radical way, before we can expect to see any reduction in the incidence of mental illness, addiction or ill health in general.

Of course, there is not much that a lone voice can do to bring about change, whether or not the truth is plain for all to see!

Thank you again for your letter, as it did give me a bit of a 'boost'.

Daniel McDwyer
Customer Service Centre
Department of Health
21-11-06

Thank you for your letter of 17-11-06, in which you state you have passed my 'email' on to The Department for Education and Skills, saying it is their responsibility for the issues I raised.

Surely, if the way we educate our young affects their health, it is the responsibility of the Department of Health to ensure that changes are made to the education system, so that it no longer poses a threat to our children's health!

Moreover, what use is the Department of Health if it shows no interest at all in the root causes of illness?

The Bury Free Press
19-11-11

We are all taught in school to make the most of our talents in anticipation of achieving the best possible rewards in the workplace. While we all need sufficient income to meet our basic needs, hopefully also with enough to enjoy a few luxuries, I suggest that lust for the acquisition of wealth or material possessions as one's main motivation in life only serves to prevent many from finding the happiness we all desire, which springs mainly from being loved by one's family, friends and acquaintances and from our capacity to love in return and to give others less fortunate as much help and support as we can. I hope teachers in schools will someday acknowledge this simple truth and focus in some degree on the spiritual needs of our young and the importance of love in relation to human happiness. Given the fierce competition involved, many of our young fail at some point in their quest for 'success' in obtaining a lucrative career, often leading to tears - but love never fails to bring the riches we need in terms of happiness and contentment, however limited our success in achieving the goals we are set by our mentors.

by Neville Lewis

Of course in the same context a great deal depends on the quality of relationships, especially how deeply both partners' hearts are engaged before they unite and have children - a problem it seems sex and relationships classes in schools signally fail to address with any success.

Mark Richmond
UNESCO

I understand you have issued new guidelines for sex education in schools on behalf of UNESCO. I hope you have taken into account the basic need for all children to be loved by their parents or at least to find the love of a partner during their teens - before failure in early love leads to an orgy of multiple sexual relationships or consolation in drink or drugs.

To that end, please find enclosed my views on the vexed subject of love and relationships in UK society and also the impact of pressurised education on children's health, which I hope you will read with an open mind.

The Bury Free Press
20-06-08

It has just been announced that there were nearly 200,000 abortions last year in England and Wales, the great majority in women over 16, who have the right to take whatever precautions they please.

It does seem that teaching in sex and relationships classes is simply not giving the right guidance to females on how to find the right partner before they engage in the act of sex, a decision which should never be taken lightly. The scowl on the face of some women one sees in the street and the language which some of them use tells its own story.

I have to admit I am glad I'm a man, although living alone without love or companionship can be a pain.

The Bury Free Press
10-02-07

Since the emancipation of women, we've seen the cult of 'free love', the mini-skirt and the hot-pants brigade and a huge escalation in the number of abortions throughout the UK Venerial diseases are now widespread in women, and the UK has the highest rate of teenage pregnancies in Europe. We also have growing numbers of latch-key kids since women with children invaded the workplace, which has led to an explosion of anti-social behaviour in many towns and cities, while an horrific one in ten children aged five to sixteen now have a clinically recognised mental disorder. Also, many males have been forced out of their homes on to 'the street', as married or common-law wives have moved on to new relationships, which is partly why 90% of our homeless are males..Meanwhile, a recent survey suggests that in the UK, where mothers of very young children are encouraged to go out to work and to make a 'success' of their lives, the quality of life of our children ranks bottom of the list for all countries in the developed world, with the USA coming second - two of the world's richest societies!

Of course, there are some exceptions, where women prefer to say no to promiscuous sex and take proper care of their young, rather than chase a career and somehow raise a family at the same time, while not all fathers engage in a culture of casual sex or abuse their partners. Nonetheless, it does seem that the 'empowerment' of women through education, and the associated lure of 'success', has left many children to face life without the full strength of their mother's love, with disastrous effects on their health and their future behaviour..

I suggest there is nothing wrong with compulsory education for all - as long as the emotional needs of our children come first, before "education, education, education!"

The Bury Free Press
23-12-09

To my mind the mark of a man lies less in his courage or fighting spirit than in his kindness to others, his love of the truth and his genuine humility - whatever gifts he was blessed with at birth. How sad it seems that so many foolish females these days see chivalry in men as a sign of weakness, when they could never be more mistaken!

The Bury Free Press
5-10-08

I understand our society has the highest incidence of teenage pregnancies in Europe, also that more than one in ten females has a sexually transmitted disease, while last year alone nearly 200,000 abortions took place in the UK. I therefore was hardly surprised when in response to my question a middle-aged friend said, "There is no such thing as 'true love'." Nonetheless, his blunt statement made me feel sad. Whatever happened to the age of romance, when every boy's dream was to fall in love with, and marry, a virgin?

For the current situation I blame the frivolous portrayal of sex by much of the media and the abysmal failure of parents and teachers alike to assign any importance to the glorious love which comes to us all around the time of puberty I submit that such love would last a lifetime if given the chance to succeed, and in the fullness of time could heal and transform our unhealthy, fragmented society, in which more than half of relationships currently fail.

The Bury Free Press
24-08-07

There seems to be a good deal of peer pressure in our society, especially among males, for young people to experience the act of sex as soon as they can, whether or not there is any love involved.

Strange as it would seem, even rabbits are capable of sex when they reach maturity - if anything even more so than human beings!

The Bury Free Press
10-07-08

We all fall in love around the time of puberty and we can all recall the name of the loved one the rest of our lives, usually with nostalgic regret at having seen our love fail, the most precious and lasting love that we know.

Given the regrettable fact that most of the knowledge we gain in school is soon lost to memory through lack of use, and also the unpalatable truth that our children are reckoned to be the most unhappy children in Europe, is not success in love more important than education, education, education?

What else do we seek if not to be happy? So where are the youth clubs in Bury where children can meet with the opposite sex and have innocent fun - instead of the seedy night clubs for those who have failed in love?

Anatomy of a Society

The Bury Free Press
20-03-08

The huge spate of abortions in the UK, and the alarming fact that we have the highest rate for teenage pregnancies in Europe, suggests that our females are just as interested in 'sex for the sake of it' as many sex-hungry, promiscuous males.

Do our teachers not recognise or stress the importance of 'true love' in our young, which comes to us all in our teens, and that it is better by far for coitus to take place as the natural consummation of love?

Promiscuity often wrecks lives, but true love, once formed, goes on and on and is the best possible basis for happy, lasting relationships. Sadly, what chance do our children have to find love when so many, as one newspaper put it, are "tested to destruction" by our pernicious, pressurised system of education?

Gordon Brown MP
Prime Minister
6-3-08

I recently heard that a Housing Association tenant has been issued with a court order that he must quit the property within 30 days if he fails to remove all the rubbish and worn-out appliances from his garden. If he fails to respond and becomes homeless, he could of course die from hypothermia, and it would cost a good deal to dispose of his body. On the other hand, if he survives but becomes ill, just as I did, the NHS and Social Services will bear the cost of his care. (I understand, on good authority, that it takes a year to recover for every month spent 'sleeping rough' on the street.)

A simple solution would be for the local Council to step in and remove the offending appliances and pass on the cost to the Housing Association and thence to the tenant, but I presume that the local Council will only collect large items on payment up front, as is the rule with my own local Council..

It does seem that every department of local and central government has its own remit to function at minimal cost, with no thought of the cost to the taxpayer when they fail to consult with each other.

It is the same, of course, when our children, as one newspaper put it, are "tested to destruction" - and the NHS and Social Services are obliged to pick up the pieces and pick up the bill.

The Bury Free Press
30-08-09

Since their emancipation, women have been schooled and hardened to forsake their motherly role in the home and take their place in the workplace. Children suffer, of course, but no-one seems to mind. As long as they get a 'full and rounded' education, which is their right, or conversely their obligation, it doesn't matter at all.

Parents and teachers seldom stop to ask the children if they enjoy the learning process. Examinations are stressful, but only for the child. Parents and teachers can wait to applaud or commiserate at their leisure. It's a race to the finish, with the nagging suspicion that if you should 'fail' you are 'finished' once and for all It's easy to see why some of our young commit suicide, with family breakdown and pressurised education combining to bring them down. With Mum out at work, Dad gone off and grandma stuck in the 'home', there's no-one to hear their anger and hurt or that lonely voice inside.

But that doesn't matter. As long as Mum can keep in work and keep the economy going, it doesn't matter a damn. There's no time to deal with children's feelings and the only hearing they get is before the magistrates when they misbehave. Output and efficiency are everything and the way you feel is nothing to anyone.

Women traditionally are the main source of goodness and love. Without love we are nothing.

The Daily Mail
15-6-11

How can we expect more care for the sick to take place in the home, when frequently no-one is there? Does not government policy encourage mothers of very young children to leave their offspring in subsidised nurseries so they can pursue a career, while many females, who would prefer to stay at home looking after their families, are forced to remain in work because of the high cost of housing, fuelled in part by their own earnings?

Since the exodus of most females from the home into the workplace and the seemingly welcome increase in GDP, I suggest it is stress which is the main cause of such things as the high incidence of asthma in children and early addiction to drink or drugs and that comfort eating, to alleviate stress, is the root cause of the growing threat of obesity, in a society which imposes more pressure on its members than ever it did when I was a boy 60 years ago, when people in general, despite being much poorer, seemed much happier than they are now!

Prime Minister
7-11-08

Astute politicians have pointed out that there are 600,000 job vacancies in England waiting to be filled, with the clear implication that all those who live on the dole don't want to work. If that is the case, why don't we compel some of the lazy scroungers to take on the jobs concerned and force the remaining million or so to get on their bikes to find work, even if the nearest job which may still be available is a hundred miles down the road? I am so pleased also to hear of the latest moves to get our so-called 'sick' back into work. Why should they wax fat on incapacity benefit, as if they were really ill, instead of bone idle?

As for new mothers who want and expect maternity leave, what is wrong with the crèche or the 'Sure Start' system, which give every mother the chance to remain in work and contribute to the economy? Surely too many stay in the home so they can suckle their young, which is simply too easy an option.

Finally, why should retired people relax and do nothing to help the economy? There is always something an old person can do to help, even if all he may do is to spend an extra hour in bed every day to save on heating. Also, why should the latest projected retirement age stop at 68? As long as a person can put one foot in front of the other without falling over, he surely is capable of work

Output and efficiency are everything, so what does it matter if some people can't live in a world without love, and so take the easy way out?

by Neville Lewis

Wendy Gordon
Department for Work and Pensions
25-08-07

Thank you for your letter of 23rd August 2007, in which you state that the Government "expects lone parents with older children to start considering entering the labour market." - meaning, of course, they will be compelled by even greater financial hardship, as benefit is cut, to go out to work as soon as their youngest child reaches the age of seven.

I suggest that many lone parents would indeed like to go out to work, not so much for the sake of their children, but so they can go out to night-clubs or pubs and hopefully find a new partner, if only for sex.

Nonetheless, there are a few good mothers about who are mothers before anything else and who much prefer, if circumstances allow, to be there for their children when needed, especially when they come home from school feeling angry or very distressed, perhaps after having been bullied at school or on their way home.

Surely we have enough latch-key children already - sometimes with catastrophic results!

The Bury Free Press
14-08-07

I understand that a new law is proposed which will force single mothers to go out to work as soon as their youngest child reaches the age of seven, in order to save the taxpayer some money. I wonder how some of our children will feel when they see their peers going home at the usual time, while they have to stay on with 'carers' till six while their Mums are still out at work. I for one used to be pleased as heck when school was over each day and I was free from the restraints of the classroom and FREE to go home and do as I please!
Do we or don't we care how our children FEEL, nor worry or give a damn how much PRESSURE we put on their Mums, especially those who love being mothers and really care for their young and how happy they are for the whole of their lives?

Furthermore, care and respect for each other as adults, as well as our general health and well-being, depends more than anything else on how well we are loved when we are young and especially during the difficult years of our teens.

I submit there is simply no price we can place on a mother's love.

To Mrs Mellerick
Dept for Work and Pensions
1-09-07

Thank you for your letter of 30th August 2007.

I see the dreadful measures proposed to encourage lone parents to go out to work as a further erosion of the role of the family, which is so vital to the stability and health of any 'society' worthy of the name - as opposed to an amorphous collection of self-seeking groups and individuals, where the weak go to the wall.

Perhaps you might like to read my final letter on the subject, a copy of which I enclose, but which no doubt will never reach Gordon Brown.

You will be relieved to know I am not on the internet, so I cannot engage in any further debate on the matter - not that it would be of any avail.

The Bury Free Press
12-12-08

It would be nice if our politicians were human and caring enough to allow single Mums living on benefit to take care of their young for at least the first seven years of their lives, which are crucial to their emotional development and well-being in later life. I was shocked and appalled to hear of the latest draconian proposal to force such mothers to prepare for work as soon as their youngest child is just one year into its life, on pain of losing their benefit.

I utterly deplore such a senseless and woefully short-sighted decision and I am frankly ashamed to be a member of a society which tolerates such cold-blooded and callous behaviour by those who are elected to govern for the common good.

The Bury Free Press
2-2-07

There is nothing quite like a mother's love and of course the child knows it. Yet many devoted mothers are forced to scrimp and scrape on low income for years, just because they prefer not to chase a career while their children are young.

Surely, these are the real heroines of our society - not the rich or famous, who often

place their children with child-minders and seldom see them all day.
A mother's love is more precious than gold, and every happy, healthy child knows it.

My own mother lived to be ninety-one, but I was still heart-broken when she died.

The Bury Free Press
1-08-08

Since their emancipation, women have excelled in every department apart from love. Girls do better than boys in exams and there are more female than male millionaires in our society today. The convenience of the crèche, and such things as child care in schools from eight until six, have enabled mothers of very young children to go out to work and pursue a career.

It is therefore hardly surprising to learn that our children are the most unhappy and overweight children in Europe, deprived as they often are of a mother's love during their formative years. As a result, even peaceful Bury St Edmunds has I am sure seen an increase in anti-social behaviour in recent years, as young boys and girls go out at week-ends in their droves to get drunk in our bars and night-clubs, often mouthing foul language in anger, the girls just as bad as the boys. . .

If a woman would rather be out at work than be a devoted, full-time mother, it would surely be better not to have children at all.

The Bury Free Press

If our young are to enjoy a carefree childhood and youth, their education needs to be free from all worries or concerns. If homework was optional and formal exams were abolished, with no fear of failing at the last hurdle after years of protracted effort, they would surely have a much greater chance to be carefree and happy, which is their right and the least they deserve.

The future for anyone is always uncertain, but fear of 'failing' or 'falling behind', in a process intended to benefit all, is surely the last thing our children need for their ongoing health and well-being.

Anatomy of a Society

Val Shiels
Dept for Children,
Schools and Families
8-2-08

Thank you for your letter of 5th February, 2008, in which you state that "regular homework gives pupils the opportunity to practise tasks done in class at home and helps them to become confident and independent in their learning - which will help throughout their time at school and in later life,"

I don't doubt that for many children this is patently true, but for many others, where there is little or no love between their parents and in some cases physical violence, home is the last place on earth as a suitable environment for study and personal development - bearing in mind the simple fact that more than 50% of relationships in our society fail.

In my case, my parents were always at war, throughout my childhood and youth, which badly affected my concentration while struggling with homework. As a result, I became more and more angry and depressed and suffered a serious breakdown at the age of 21, which put paid to my university career and destroyed any real chance of forming a happy, successful relationship. Had I been free from the burden of homework, I would have been able to socialise more with my peers and escape much more frequently from an extremely stressful home environment. I might even have been successful in love, which is more important to me than all the knowledge I ever obtained in school or college and all I have ever learned since!

The Bury Free Press
12-12-07

I cannot see why any children should have to struggle all evening with homework, day after day, year on year, while their parents can sit back and relax watching TV. Our government is at last talking about giving more choices to children and easing some of the pressures upon them, because they are so unhappy. Most working parents are free to decide how much overtime they do. Surely our children, who have less stamina than adults, deserve the same option, if they are ever to be happy at all.

by Neville Lewis

The Bury Free Press
3-07-08

I hate hearing proud females boasting about their achievements in school. Females are much stronger emotionally than males, and therefore cope better than boys with the stress of exams.

It would be nice, nonetheless, to hear how many girls get good results in the more testing sciences, which require the application of logic - an attribute I regret I have seldom found in a woman!

The Bury Free Press
19-08-08

I shall never understand how one can be deemed to have 'qualified' in any aspect of learning, and it seems to me that the grim struggle for adequate 'qualifications' actually restricts and inhibits the learning process. Surely teacher assessments and self-recommending samples of class-work, rather than formal tests which end in the huge hurdle of 'final' exams, would lead to far higher levels of learning as well as an ongoing thirst for knowledge and expertise long after school or college is over.

Furthermore, fear of 'failure', which also blights the learning process, would be entirely removed and many suicides in our impressionable young prevented.

The Bury Free Press
1-6-07

I am curious to know what our politicians mean by "social mobility", bearing in mind, as a developed society, we all depend on each other for our survival, and we need storemen, shop assistants, lorry-drivers and refuse-collectors, etc etc, much more than we need graduates in golf-course management or media studies, or surveys into the sex-life of marsupials...

Baroness Williams
15-8-11

Thank you so much for your lovely letter, which I received today.

For the sake of more social cohesion, I hope you agree we should acknowledge the truth that as a society we all depend on each other, not just for the creation of wealth but for our very survival, whether we work as a top executive in an international company or as a humble factory worker producing the goods we all need to survive, with equal respect accorded to all.

Perhaps we should place less emphasis in our schools on 'social mobility' and focus more on the need to master the 3 R's and then to help all of our young to prepare for work which suits their many and varied talents. We should never induce the feeling in impressionable children that somehow they have 'missed out' or 'failed' in the chase for 'success'. Thankfully, many in any case are perfectly happy to do the menial but vital tasks on which we all depend for our ongoing health and security, as long as their jobs are secure, while there are always opportunities later in life for those who are motivated to further their education and chances for greater financial reward for their particular talents.

The Times
11-06-08

In response to the latest statistics on poverty in our society, I suggest there will always be large numbers of people living in relative poverty as long as we continue to reward our workforce in an hierarchical way, with priority given to the professional and managerial classes and those with special skills which require training, such as our engineers, carpenters and plumbers etc.

In the nature of things, we also need unskilled workers in shops, stores and factories, and many other locations, doing simple, repetitive tasks, such as filling shelves or collecting our refuse, without whom society would collapse.

It therefore seems to me disingenuous and morally indefensible for our politicians to suggest that the only way out of poverty for our low-paid, unskilled workers, on whom we depend for our very survival, is to train for better-paid work. Why don't Government Ministers admit it is greed which stands in the way of a more equitable distribution of wealth in societies like ours?

by Neville Lewis

The Bury Free Press
1-6-11

In the mad scramble for places at university, students are set demanding and stressful exams to make it easy for professors and teachers to pick the best brains from the bag, leaving the rest to be deemed to have 'failed'. As for course work, some students are so anxious to 'succeed' that they even cheat, culling essays from the internet and passing them off as their own. At the same time there is widespread concern about standards not being met in some schools.

Such a fiercely competitive system and the setting of arbitrary standards is clearly counter-productive as well as starkly unjust in its cruel selection procedures. No-one who has done his best should ever be deemed to have 'failed', while standards would rise to undreamed-of heights if learning took place on a collaborative, rather than a competitive basis. Have not huge advances in medical science taken place due to collaborative work and shared knowledge between nations? Surely the same culture should apply in our schools and colleges, which would not only raise overall standards, but also encourage an ethos of care and concern for each other as human beings, the most valuable bonus of all.

The Rt Hon David Cameron
Prime Minister
1-6-11

Why does there need to be such a thing as a degree or diploma, a pass or a failure to obtain such a 'qualification'? We all obtain a degree of knowledge at school or college, while many who fail to obtain a 'superlative' classification cope with a job in the same genre and at the same level as someone with letters after his name - sometimes even much better.

Just as a prime minister uses his judgement to select his cabinet, the best judge of anyone's abilities is surely his teachers or his employer. Do we not ask for a reference from an employer or former teacher when we move on to another job? What can be wrong with professors or teachers doing the same in school or college, rather than put so much intense pressure on young people to 'perform' in exams?

When we confer artificial degrees or diplomas, while 'failing' others with almost equal ability, we create symbolic social and economic divisions which can last for a lifetime, despite our alleged aim for a just and caring society. Churchill failed to get a degree, but will always be revered for his outstanding degree of courage and his inspiring leadership at a desperate time for the whole nation. Surely there is a lesson in that!

Anatomy of a Society

The Daily Mail
11-6-11

When I was a lad of fourteen, I thoroughly enjoyed doing a paper-round in the morning and delivering groceries in the late afternoon after school. I was immensely pleased to have money to spend which I had earned, as well as the tips I received from kind-hearted customers, especially at Christmas time!

There are many young boys and girls, who once they have mastered the three 'R's, show little interest in further study in any particular field and who would sooner leave school early and enter the workplace, providing work was available, without wasting more of their own and their teachers' time. Much of the knowledge they struggle to gain is soon lost to memory and never needed again and most would be happy doing unskilled but vital tasks in our shops, stores and factories etc, without whom we would not survive. Meanwhile, we have blinkered intellectuals in government who think it necessary to know every detail of every child's progress at every stage of their learning career, as if education was all that mattered in life, particularly when we are young, no matter how stressful it may be for some. Diversity is a function of human nature and all creation, which is just as well for all our sakes, as few would wish to clean hospitals or offices or collect refuse etc etc - services which nonetheless are vital to health - if everyone wanted to learn a particular skill which required years of training, or indeed to become a university professor!

By the same token, given the premise that there will, in the nature of things, always be diverse levels of learning in different schools, the current obsession with statistics and constant attempts, at huge cost in terms of time, effort and money, to bring all our schools into line, are surely utterly pointless and futile! Such a crazy procedure is also harmful to health, given the painful, gratuitous pressures involved, for teachers and pupils alike, which not all, but many find hard or impossible to bear, as teachers freely admit.

The Bury Free Press
07-01-11

Dear Sir,

The continuing scandal of huge bankers' bonuses and massive rises in business executives' salaries, at a time when most people are having to tighten their belts, clearly shows we are a million miles away from becoming a truly caring, sharing society.

by Neville Lewis

Early influences tend to dictate the way we behave as we journey through life and as we have trained our children's minds to be centred on self-aggrandisement, so we have become a nation of self-seeking individuals, with little concern for the needs of the family, in a society where sadly a third of the population live on their own, some with no-one to turn to in time of need.

While we will always need enterprise to create wealth, it is simply not possible to worship the god of mammon and the God of Love at the same time. Therefore we need to see change in the way we set goals for our young in our schools, teaching our children that it is better to give than to receive and that sometimes the smallest act of kindness can bring joy to a lonely heart. Only then can we expect to obtain the happy, truly caring society which our privileged governing plutocracy ironically hopes to achieve by a pie in the sky act of faith.

Ann Talboys HMI
Divisional Manager
Quality Assurance
OFSTED
22-7-11

Thank you for your letters in response to mine regarding our system of education. I note that you seem reluctant to mention the little word, 'love', which propitiously comes to us all in our teens and which if successful, could potentially change the lives of many children who come from disturbed or broken relationships. Sadly, such love usually fails, partly because of the pressures of education, which often stand in the way and leave little time to pursue the needs of the heart. As a result, countless young boys and girls are left broken-hearted, who then go on to express their growing appetite for sex based on superficial attraction - a scenario which to the best of my knowledge is never discussed in our schools with our young .And so, tragically, the current cycle of widespread disturbed or broken relationships continues, with its sad impact on the emotional well-being and subsequent wayward behaviour of many young people in later years.

I cannot see how any inspectorate can judge how children feel deep inside, especially if all they really long for is to be loved if they are deeply unhappy at home. I am also convinced if there was more love in our soulless, self-seeking society, standards of learning in schools would rise to undreamed-of heights and the futile and hugely costly attempts to compel teachers to achieve better results, by such means as odious league tables, would be recognised for their crass stupidity, in a world where differences of ability in all walks of life are a function of human nature and will remain so, however much we constantly struggle to bring all our schools up to the same average and arbitrary standard.

Do you know that the number of people in our gaols is now at the highest level ever recorded, around 94,000, which takes no account of the thousands who escape detection and prosecution for their dishonest behaviour? Honesty and empathy for others are naturally associated with love - the love which sadly falls short of the need for so many of our young in our society today. A lack of love, especially in early life, is also surely the main reason why one in four of our population suffer the horrors of mental illness at some point in their lives. Why on earth does OFSTED believe it is possible to train our young to become caring, honest citizens, with a healthy, positive outlook on life, if there is no love in their lives, while at the same time we subject them to intense psychological pressure to make the maximum use of their talents before the 'opportunity' slips away? The proof of the pudding lies in the widespread habit of comfort eating to alleviate stress and the growing problem of obesity!

The Bury Free Press
21-01-09

As every new generation of teachers enters our schools, in the nature of things some will be better at teaching than others. At the same time, again in the nature of things, social and economic factors affecting pupils' performance will always be subject to change as the years go by. It therefore seems to me stupid and pointless to keep striving to bring all our schools into line - at great cost in terms of money and teaching time. League tables, which lie at the core of the 'system', must damage morale in low-scoring schools and breed complacency in high-scoring schools, and therefore should surely be scrapped, along with compulsory homework and stressful, time-wasting formal exams, which cause deep anxiety in some of our young.

Freed from gratuitous pressures, our children would then have a far better chance of a happy, carefree childhood, which must benefit their health, while teachers' health would also improve and fewer would leave the profession. Paradoxically, I also believe that such changes would herald a passion for learning not seen before in our young.

by Neville Lewis

Val Shiels
*Public Communications Unit
Dept for children, schools and families
14-01-08*

Thank you for your letter of 11th January, 2008, in reply to mine dated 12th December 2007. In your letter, you mention the optimum, quite modest time that our children should start spending each week doing schoolwork at home, increasing according to age, as recommended by Government. Although you also state that homework isn't compulsory, but rather an option for each individual school, let's not be disingenuous about this, as we all know that homework is, in practice, compulsory for the vast majority of children in schools.

I think you must also concede, if you are honest, that a great many children spend a great deal of time fretting and worrying over their homework, often because their concentration is affected by problems at home or by bullying, which is known to be rife in our schools. (I take it the Government is aware of the facts regarding domestic violence and broken relationships in our society today, and the numbers of children also affected by bullying.) I submit that in consequence a great many children spend a much longer time struggling to deal with their homework than the time that is recommended as "good practice" by Government. Meanwhile, of course, there are bound to be teachers who are over-zealous in the amounts of homework they set, as they themselves are under great pressure to get 'good results', because of obnoxious 'league tables', which can affect their security and their careers.

The net result of such pressures has been a generation of children bingeing on food for comfort from stress, which in turn has led to a major health problem, in the form of widespread obesity, for doctors to cope with in years to come - at huge cost to the NHS. We also know that mental health problems, which hit one in four people at some point in their lives, frequently start with anxiety, essentially due to a 'lack of love' and too much pressure in early life. Surely the sanest, best policy would be to scrap odious league tables, which don't always reflect the ability of teachers to teach, and to make homework optional by statute for all our children, both for the sake of our teachers' as well as their pupils' ongoing mental and physical health. I could be wrong, but I suspect standards would actually rise, as children arrived back in school every day feeling refreshed and eager to learn. Children are only young once, so they have only one chance to enjoy a happy, carefree childhood, free from the gratuitous worries or fears induced by our pressurised system of education.

I hope this clarifies my position on homework and also league tables for schools.

Anatomy of a Society

The Child Support Agency
17-12-07

As new generations of teachers and pupils enter our schools, in the nature of things some will be better or worse that those they replace, both in the ability of teachers to motivate, and in the range of ability in every new intake of children, so some inequalities between schools will always exist

For that reason, apart from ensuring that no child is disadvantaged through poverty, and that new teaching methods which prove useful are passed on to all schools, I see no sense in forever attempting to bring all our schools into line. League tables put severe pressure on teachers and children alike, but for the best results motivation should surely come from within, as children develop their individual and varied abilities - without the distraction of having to focus on subjects which may not appeal or attract their ongoing interest.

Surveys have also shown that excessive pressure can be counter-productive and harmful to health, which no doubt is one of the reasons why one in four people suffer some form of mental ill health at some point in their lives - at huge cost to the NHS and our Social Services. In an ideal world, I suggest there would be no such thing as pressurised education, but standards would leap to undreamed-of heights as children followed their natural aims and aptitudes. Teachers would be more switched-on and happy, not having to push or cajole, or fill in voluminous forms, and a whole new spirit would come to our schools, with learning a joy and a pleasure for all - no tears, no fear of failure, no breakdowns ever again!

David Cameron MP
Prime Minister
14-12-11

Why on earth do we think it necessary to send so many of our young to University? Does it not frequently give expectations and prospects of senior positions in our society which are simply not available or attainable for the majority? Meanwhile a degree in such things as Latin, English Literature, Philosophy or History, much less a degree in Media Studies or Golf Course Management, can scarcely contribute much to the production and supply of useful goods and services for public consumption, on which every economy depends for the creation of wealth.

We may always need a tiny minority of well-educated intellectuals, skilled in oratory, at the highest levels of our society - but much more importantly, we will always need huge numbers of skilled, unskilled and semi-skilled workers in shops, stores and factories etc to produce and distribute the wealth that we need, without which we would have no health service, no banks, no police force or penal system or system of education - indeed no society at all as we know it today!

Happy Christmas!

The Bury Free Press
22-11-06

May I ask who is more important: the educated woman who has found that promiscuous marsupials tend to produce stronger young than their less promiscuous relations - as reported on BBC Radio 4; or the man who strives to keep his family together when his partner has been unfaithful - bearing in mind the increasing incidence of sexually transmitted disease?

Paul Lewis
Moneybox
BBC Radio 4
18-02-08

I am convinced we will never see a real 'global economy' until the impediments to trade between nations are completely removed. Fluctuating currency values between separate states are clearly bad for trade, so a common global currency, which may take years to achieve, would nonetheless entirely remove such problems as the balance of trade and indebtedness between nation states, while concerns over a rise in the cost of imports would disappear altogether, as there wouldn't be such things as imports or exports, nor any need for a 'manufacturing base' for each individual state.

Meanwhile, if the spurious concept that trading in money can somehow make more money, by attracting interest, was abandoned - because all interest has to be earned by people's labour - there would be no need to juggle with interest rates in a desperate balancing act to ward off inflation and at the same time prevent a recession.

All business depends on trust. If I place an order for goods or work to be done by a company, the company assumes I will pay when I get their invoice, after the work has been done or the goods supplied, and if I pay 'up front' for an item, I naturally trust it will be delivered.

Further to the principle of trust, I see nothing wrong with banks lending money to individuals or companies with no interest attached, as I believe has been practised successfully by Moslems for many years. After all, few people wish to be blacklisted for credit in this day and age, and banks have the right to charge for the costs they incur in chasing people for late payment of debt.

Finally, as I hope you agree, we need to stop gambling with company capital on all the stock markets around the world, before any real and lasting stability can be obtained for business to flourish and people worldwide to prosper. We might have to sacrifice short-term profit for long-term gain, but such a change would surely be of great benefit to our children and their children in years to come.

I suggest there could be no better time than the present to make a start by freezing interest on loans worldwide, thereby bringing a huge boost to the global economy and thereby an end to the current recession.

Paul Lewis
Money Box
BBC Radio 4
24-09-08

I shall never understand why the success and stability of the global economy should have to depend on such a fragile and fickle component as 'confidence'. Surely our politicians and leaders of industry throughout the world should have learned by now that it is simply too risky and dangerous for the means of exchange and company capital to be traded for profit on an open market, which inevitably leads to the 'boom and bust' cycle with which we are all too familiar.

I see nothing wrong with free enterprise or investment which hopes for a return, as demonstrated so well by the programme, 'The Dragons' Den', but I cannot condone the principle of interest on loans which has led to such a reckless lending spree by so many banks and financial institutions in recent years and the resultant mountain of bad debt which has triggered the current crisis. As I have stated before, only work can make money and all interest has to be paid for by someone's labour, so there is no magic formula whereby we could all become millionaires and live on the interest from our earnings without ever working again!

by Neville Lewis

Paul Lewis
Moneybox
BBC Radio 4
10-01-09

I understand that the Wall Street Crash which triggered the Great Depression of the thirties was caused by a boom in share prices followed by a wave of selling for profit, which in turn led to panic selling as share prices plummeted. As we all know, the current economic crisis began when the banks' lending spree in the housing market got out of hand and led to a mountain of bad debt and the ensuing crippling 'credit crunch', as banks everywhere fought to survive their own reckless profiteering policies. We are now informed that one man was able to milk 'the system' to the tune of 50 billion dollars, which surely suggests there is something seriously wrong with 'the system'!

I appreciate I am not alone in thinking we must have a radical change in economic policies before the damaging cycle of 'boom and bust' happens again and the world is plunged yet again into another severe recession. Please find attached my previous letter, in which I have tried to explain the changes which I believe need to take place to obtain, in the fullness of time, real economic stability and an end to 'boom and bust' once and for all.

As stated in my earlier letter, I see interest on the means of exchange as a deterrent to enterprise and a burden to the community at large, with the only real winners in good times the banks, while trading in multiple currencies and company capital on the open market, where a loss of volatile 'confidence' can have disastrous results, should somehow be brought to an end.

The Economist
23-01-08

Is it not time that the world's banks stopped playing ducks and drakes with the money supply? Greed for profit is the sole reason why banks are now catching a cold from reckless lending to people who cannot repay, so now as a direct result the whole global economy faces a possible major recession.

If banks cannot take proper care of our money, who can? I submit that only work can make money, so gambling with people's earnings should surely stop, with all banks and finance companies who deal with the means of exchange being non-profit-making institutions, providing a service with no crippling interest on loans and just charging fees to cover their costs.

The Third World states are a huge potential market for Western goods, but I once read that for every dollar of 'aid' that the United States gives, thirteen dollars comes back in interest on loans! Of course, if we were all millionaires, like some bank executives, we could all live off the interest, so no-one would need to work?

If gambling with company capital on stock exchanges around the world also ceased, I submit we would then have a firm and secure base on which world trade could flourish and grow, while genuine aid, in terms of money and expertise, from the rich to the poorer states, would bring even more wealth in return.

The Guardian
18-12-09

I once read in an American magazine that for every dollar of aid donated by the USA to the impoverished Third World states, 13 dollars comes back by way of interest on loans! Bearing in mind that shariah law prohibits the charging of interest on loans, perhaps this helps explain why the World Trade Centre became a prime target for Moslem extremists in their horrific attack on 'the land of the free' in 2001.

I suspect that Adam Smith, who promoted the concept that self-interest was the key to the creation of wealth, could not have known at the time that self-interest would change to obsessive greed and that a huge gap would emerge between rich and poor in developed as well as developing countries around the world. It is worth noting that interest on loans siphons huge sums of money from ordinary, hard-working people into the pockets of bankers and financial 'experts' with little real work involved and I submit that as long as greed and its counterpart, corruption, persist, the prospect of 'peace on earth and good will to men' will remain an impossible dream.

The National Institute of Economic and Social Research
12-12-07

I understand that the Wall Street Crash, which triggered the Great Depression of the thirties, was caused by an unprecedented boom in share prices, followed by a wave of selling for profit, which escalated into panic selling as share prices plummeted.

Is it not time that the global economy was given a firmer footing by bringing an end to trading in volatile stocks and shares on the open market? Have we not seen again, with the dreadful Northern Rock crisis, how a sharp fall in public 'confidence' can have disastrous results?

by Neville Lewis

At the same time it would surely make sense to work towards a common global currency, which would bring an end to constant concerns over comparative currency values and nightmare scenarios such as Black Wednesday, when the value of the pound in everyone's pocket was cut at a stroke.

The two simple changes suggested would surely bring lasting stability to the global economy and thereby, in the fullness of time, greater prosperity for all.

The Times
25-09-10

I hope you agree that it is simply not true that speculative trading in the financial markets by many banks really brings wealth to a nation. Yes, companies need investment to prosper, but the option to sell on a whim for profit often brings serious economic instability and sometimes wrecks the companies which really generate wealth, as is starkly illustrated by the catastrophic Wall Street Crash, which was caused by a boom in share prices followed by a rush to sell for profit. The fall of Lehman Brothers and the recent banking crisis again highlights the same recurring problem, which surely has to be addressed and resolved by world leaders across the globe if we are to avoid future boom and bust crises with their devastating effects on the lives of so many people. To generate stability, we surely also must work towards a single global currency, bearing in mind the damaging impact on trade and industry of constant fluctuations in currency values fuelled by speculative trading in multiple currencies on the open market.. After all, the invention of money was intended to facilitate the exchange of goods and services in complex economies, not to make a number of clever financial entrepreneurs extremely rich!

Finally, I see no reason why banks, or indeed private companies, should be allowed to accumulate huge sums of money by charging interest on loans. I know this has been the bedrock of traditional banking across the world - except in Muslim societies - for many centuries, and that banks have always been profit-making concerns, allegedly providing a service to the wider community. Our excellent NHS provides a service, so why should the world's banks not provide a similar service run by the state in the same way, without charging interest, which I consider to be ill-gotten gain? Viable companies often fail due to crippling rates of interest on loans, while many new ventures fail to get off the ground for the same reason, as we all know. Interest is a dead weight which stifles enterprise in the real wealth-creating world of work and also inflates prices of goods in our shops and only brings wealth to those at the top of the banking community - not to the nation itself. I therefore submit that the whole system needs radical change, with banks worldwide made an arm of the state and no longer run for profit. Was it not reckless lending for profit in the housing market which triggered the recent recession? To those who say that interest on loans has to be charged as a lever to make people repay, I would strongly suggest that no-one in this day and age can wish to be black-listed for credit or taken to court for debt and declared bankrupt. Of course there is always some risk when a loan is offered, just as there is some risk that an expensive hospital operation may fail. As for bankers' bonuses, if bonuses are to be paid at all, I suggest they should be based only on a bank's success in achieving low levels of bad debt, while offering the best possible service to the public at large - a genuine service where the needs of the community come first.

The Economist
2-8-11

I am convinced if banks were no longer run for profit, their operations funded by the state, and if interest on loans was strictly banned, the benefits to business and consumers worldwide would far outweigh the cost to tax-payers. The truth is that only work in the production and supply of useful goods and services can create wealth, while history has shown us again and again that trading in money for profit can only lead to uncertainty and frequent pauses or downturns in economic activity, sometimes lasting for years.

Loans to give impetus to new enterprise and growth in the creation of wealth would continue, with no interest needed as an incentive to repay, as no-one in this day and age - nor indeed any nation state - can wish to be black-listed for credit. At the same time, if speculative trading for profit in company capital on the open market, which we know can also lead to damaging cycles of 'boom and bust', was also banned, and a common global currency established, even greater economic stability would ensue, with every chance for trade and industry to flourish as never before.

Such radical changes would, of course, require global political consensus and a willingness by governments worldwide to forgo short-term national interests in favour of long-term, sustained growth in the global economy, ultimately leading to greater prosperity for all. Given the current crisis of national debt facing some countries, with its inherent risks to the global economy, I see no reason why a sustained effort by leaders worldwide should not be capable of bringing about the far-reaching and worthwhile changes I have described, which would give countries with huge deficits a far better chance of repaying their debts - at the same time reducing the risks to the global economy of a potentially serious default.

by Neville Lewis

The Economist
27-9-11

I hope you agree that one hardly needs to be a rocket scientist to appreciate that wealth can only be created by the production and supply of useful goods and services for public consumption, while gambling for profit with the means of exchange frequently leads to downturns in economic growth or major recessions, such as were caused by the Wall Street Crash and the recent banking crisis.

Surely it is time the whole banking system around the world was no longer run for profit, but funded by tax-payers as an arm of the state, providing a free service to both business and consumers and thereby creating the stability needed for sustained growth throughout the global economy. As long as we cling to the spurious notion that trading in money for profit can somehow make more money, I see no end to damaging cycles of 'boom and bust', which blight economic growth and cause misery and hardship to millions of people across the world. Why it is mine is the only voice expressing this simple truth?

As long as banks lend for profit, there will always be governments willing to borrow for political gain and recurring crises caused by unsustainable debt, with its disastrous effects both on the banks and the wider economy, the cost to shore up the banks being met by the working community engaged in the creation of wealth. A tax on bankers' bonuses by one individual nation is no answer to a global problem, which requires statesmen of the highest callable to bring about much-needed radical change to a deeply flawed financial system, where banks continue to suck the life-blood from a supine, acquiescent public.

The Economist
7-12-10

If trading in company capital on the open market was banned, there could be no more 'boom and bust' cycles caused by dramatic changes in fickle 'confidence'. If banks were no longer run for profit, there could be no more catastrophes caused by reckless profiteering policies in the banking community. If interest on loans, which is a major deterrent to enterprise and produces nothing of value, was banned, business would receive a huge boost. Finally, if a common global currency was established, the benefits to international trade would be enormous.

The only barrier to such changes is the popular delusion that trading in money can somehow make more money, when in fact such a trade is a parasite which feeds on the flesh of the real world of work and by its nature resists all efforts to treat or control it.

Robert Peston
BBC TV
15-2-10

It seems to me that boom and bust cycles have all had their origins in the financial services sector, from the Wall Street Crash and the Great Depression of the 30's to the present banking crisis which has affected the whole of the world.

The truth is that only work can make money and all interest has to be paid by people's labour. As long as banks are allowed to charge interest on loans and as long as we cling to the spurious concept that trading in money can somehow make more money, I submit we will continue to have damaging boom and bust cycles and huge sums of money sucked at will by the banking community from those who are engaged in the real world of work - i.e. the production and supply of useful goods and services.

I hope someday the leaders of industry and governments worldwide will acknowledge the need for all banks to be non-profit-making institutions providing a free service funded by the state, for interest on loans and trading in company capital on an open market to be banned and for a common global currency to be established as soon as possible. I submit that such changes would be a huge boost to trade and industry throughout the world and bring an end to boom and bust once and for all.

At the same time, of course, an end would come to the farcical scandal of bankers' bonuses, while such changes would also provide a real opportunity to reduce the huge gap between rich and poor.

The Times
8-02-09

The invention of money was intended to facilitate the exchange of goods and services and in no way to be a deterrent to trade and industry with the imposition of interest on loans. Nor was it intended to broker an economic recession every few years. I submit that the management of the means of exchange should be a free service provided by banks around the world, just as our excellent health service in the UK is free for all our citizens. At the same time, it would help if the world had a single currency and if speculative trading in company capital on an open market was finally recognised as a potential source of serious financial instability and therefore was brought to an end.

How else can we expect to obtain a stable global economy and an end to the cycle of 'boom and bust'?

To our current Prime Minister
8-12-09
Mr Brown,

I note that the index of share prices in London has now risen from less than 4000 to more than 5000 and I presume it will keep rising and making fortunes for bankers and stock-brokers until boom and bust happens again and once more the banks have to be bailed out.

As a pensioner who qualifies for housing and council tax benefit, I regret I don't have the money right now to pay the 14000 pounds which I understand every person will have to find this particular time, so it will take me a good many years to find the money required at a rate of 10 pounds a week, which is all I can afford - so will you PLEASE stop this business from happening again?

To Various Members of the Establishment
17-12-11

The hidden value to the economy of a caring woman is much greater than one might think. Such a woman will ensure she remains loyal to her partner as best she can for the sake of her children, knowing how broken relationships can cause lasting harm to one's offspring. Such damage, of course, often costs our NHS and Social Services huge sums of money in terms of ongoing care.

Such a woman will also be anxious to take care of her frail, ageing parents as long as she can, rather than see them languish in a care home for the elderly, as thousands do without good cause, often at huge cost to the state. If there is room, she will, with her partner's consent, also be willing to take in and care for her ageing relatives when they can't cope living alone, thereby saving the state a great deal in terms of state-funded carers, who in their droves currently visit elderly people who cannot cope well on their own and whose families are nowhere to be seen.

Such a woman will also provide all the love and guidance her children will need to become honest, caring citizens themselves, thereby saving our police force a great deal in terms of time and money, along with our over-stretched penal system. Also such a woman, while she remains at home in her preferred role, at least gives one unemployed male a better chance to find work than would be the case if she remained in full-time employment the same as most females today, even mothers of very young children, who in turn often receive costly, state-funded 'Sure-Start' care for their young.

Finally, if the majority of females were caring enough to remain mostly at home taking care of their young and their elderly relations, there would be far fewer people living alone, less pressure on housing as a result, house prices would fall and a home would become widely affordable on one person's wage, as in times past, with no fall in most people's standard of living!

So a little more love from the female sex could go a very long way to reducing the state sector budget - not to mention improving most people's quality of life. The difficulty, of course, lies in finding such wonderful females, who sadly seem to be nearly extinct in our self-seeking society today. Clearly we are all born with love in our hearts, but its finest expression surely has always come from the hearts of the female sex.

The Guardian
7-12-11

I hate to denigrate the opposite sex, but where are the women of days gone by, who stuck by their man and stayed mainly at home to take care of their young and their elderly relatives? I have met many males in my ancient home town of Bury St Edmunds who became homeless when their relationships failed due to their partners' infidelity, also a number of young men who became ill or disturbed after being abandoned by their own mothers when they moved on to another relationship. While some males clearly behave badly, I can recall a time when such behaviour in any female was widely condemned, yet in today's world it seems to be seen as perfectly acceptable. I have met several females in recent years who said they would sooner be at home taking care of their families, but that the high cost of housing forced them to remain in work. Who, nonetheless, can really believe them, when few women would wish to relinquish their independence, while every Friday and Saturday night one sees crowds of scantily-clad females scouring our streets, clubs and pubs in search of sex?

by Neville Lewis

The change in the role of the female has of course led to the grim fact that a third of our population now live on their own, a most unnatural and often harsh situation for social animals such as ourselves, which is also the root cause of the grave shortage and high cost of housing in our society today. For me one of the saddest signs of the times was the recent appeal by the YMCA - in St Edmundsbury's publication, 'Community Spirit' - for volunteers in West Suffolk to take in homeless 16- and 17-year-olds on a temporary basis, who presumably come from homes short on love. I sincerely hope none of them dies from the winter cold before help can be found!

Copies: SANE
The Mental Health Foundation
The Royal College of GP's
The Royal College of Psychiatrists
The Medical Research Council
OFSTED
The National Association of Head Teachers
Andrew Lansley MP
Relate
BBC Radio Suffolk
The Archbishop of Canterbury
MIND

The Bury Free Press
25-02-08

While holidaying in Scotland some years ago, I happened to meet two young men from India who had been recruited to work on a mainframe computer in Glasgow. They were so lively and jocular that I was curious to know more about them.

They told me they came from a society where 95% of relationships lasted for life and that a tiny, wealthy minority, who dumped their ageing relatives into old people's homes, were treated with open scorn and contempt by the bulk of the population. They also said that mental illness is virtually unknown in their society. They openly admitted that there was such a thing as arranged marriages, but that the feelings of both parties were taken into account every time.

While I see nothing wrong with the emancipation of women and their right to live as they please, it does seem sad that the role of the female in societies like ours has changed, and also that so many relationships fail.

The result has been an explosion in numbers of people living alone - around 30% of the population of the UK, which the experts reckon is set to rise. Many others are herded together in hostels for the homeless or mentally sick, while many more languish in homes for the elderly waiting to die.

I suspect there must be hundreds, perhaps thousands of citizens who fall into one of the four categories mentioned above and who live and reside in wealthy Bury St Edmunds.

The Bury Free Press
18-02-08

I wonder how many women regard motherhood as a casual, part-time occupation while they pursue a career at the same time. I was dismayed to hear that child benefit may be cut when a second child reaches the age of seven, which puts pressure on mothers to go out to work. Surely we have enough neglected, latch-key children already, often with serious consequences in terms of anti-social behaviour and addiction to drink or drugs in years to come, not to mention the cost to the tax-payer in terms of policing, judicial and penal costs and also the NHS and Social Services...

Good, caring mothers, who devote all their lives into looking after their young to the point when they find a partner and move to a home of their own, should be richly rewarded - much more indeed than they are now. It does seem we are so anxious to prevent any abuse of 'the system' by a tiny minority, that we deny help and support to those who most need and deserve it - at a cost, in the long-term, which far exceeds any benefit to the Exchequer! ..

The British Medical Association
Copy The Police Federation
Copy The Lord Chief Justice
Copy The Home Secretary
25-02-08

The NHS and Social Services are primarily concerned with the treatment of illness as it occurs, and only retrospectively in its supposed origins. The same applies to the police, our judicial and penal systems in dealing with crime and anti-social behaviour, and no-one involved in these departments seems willing to place any blame on our pressurised system of education, nor on the failure of so many relationships in our society today.

Meanwhile, the department for children, schools and families seems only interested in seeing how well our children 'perform' under pressure, as well as advising our young that it's okay to have sex, as long as it's 'safe' and never before the age of 16.

Shakespeare once said that "the child is father of the man." As long as we choose to ignore the emotional needs of our young, I suggest that widespread poor mental health and miscreant behaviour will continue to blight our society in years to come. There is such a thing as 'true love', but who gives a damn about love any more in our self-centred, self-seeking society today? How we feel doesn't matter at all, and in matters of health or behaviour, it's much easier to blame it all on our genes or 'bad habits' like smoking or drinking!

The Times
4-02-09

A mother's love is the rock upon which every happy, caring family is built. I had a wonderful mother, who was always there when needed, and I knew I would do my utmost to 'keep my nose clean' while she was alive.

60 years ago, neighbours would help each other with basic supplies such as bread or milk, at a time when food was rationed. Doors were left unlocked at night and you could safely leave your bike in the street with no padlock or chain to protect it. You could also wander and play with no fear of being attacked or molested by strangers.

That was when I was a boy and before women invaded the workplace. 60 years on, we now have a female Home Secretary reporting that "overall crime is down."

The Bury Free Press
17-11-09

I refer to Bury Town Council's recent survey asking residents if they would like to see an increase in Council Tax to provide, among other things, more surveillance cameras and more police to patrol our streets.

If we aim to reduce crime and anti-social behaviour in Bury, I suggest a far better option would be to provide more recreational activities for young people, especially youth clubs, where children can meet with the opposite sex after school and be made to feel they are valued members of the community. Our children are our future, and if we ignore their need to socialise - and hopefully find love in someone's eyes - they may well rebel and ignore the needs of others in subsequent years.

I have long believed it is a serious mistake for teachers to insist that getting a 'good education' is all that matters when we are young, which is surely a far too narrow and bigoted view of the needs of a child!

Alan Addison
Customer Service Centre
Dept of Health
12-09-08

Thank you for your letter of 3rd September 2008 in response to mine of 19th August to the Bury Free Press, which I copied to Alan Johnson, also for sending a copy of my letter to the Department for Children Schools and Families, who, in your own words, "have responsibility for the issues raised." As expected, all I got from the Department for Children, Schools and Families was the usual 'spin' to confirm that "exams are a long established feature of school life" - as if I didn't know (!) - and that "qualifications are a ticket to further learning, employment and further educational potential" - again as if I didn't know. This means, of course, that the millions of children who fail to get five good grades at O-level GCSE have no chance of success in the stampede for money and status which grips our society today, and I hope you realise the future to those who fail must look bleak indeed!.

Do you not know that one in every ten children between the ages of five and sixteen has a clinically recognised mental disorder, which must be in part due to our absurdly pressurised system of education? Do you not also know that our children are the most unhappy and overweight children in all of Europe and that obesity poses a threat to health which is considered by doctors to be just as serious as smoking, obesity generally arising from bingeing on food for comfort from stress?

I submit it is the responsibility of your department, the Department of Health, to force the issue with the Department for Children, Schools and Families and to make education more palatable and 'user-friendly' and so bring an end once and for all to the stream of children who break under the pressure of constant homework and so many tests and exams on which so much is made to depend. Teachers know perfectly well the ability and progress of each pupil they teach, so there would be nothing wrong with teacher assessments backed up by samples of work done in class.

by Neville Lewis

Lauren Reid
Customer Service Centre
Dept of Health
6-10-08

Thank you for your letter of 26-09-2008 in response to mine to Alan Addison of 12th September.

I suspect that any policies by Government to offer so-called 'healthier' foods and more opportunities for children to exercise, well-intended as they may be, will probably have only minimal impact on the future health of our young, simply because, as the saying goes, 'you can take a horse to water, but you can't make it drink!'

I know my ideas with regard to our system of education are radical and controversial, but I am convinced that most mental and physical illness is mainly caused by emotional stress due to a 'lack of love', especially in early life, and too much pressure in school.

From my own experience of mental illness and alcoholism, I am quite sure that a happy, carefree childhood is crucial to good mental and physical health in later years. In my case my parents were always at war throughout my childhood and youth, making me angry inside and very depressed. As a result, I suffered a serious attack of anxiety and depression at the age of 21, which cut short my university career. I also had a severe heart attack in my fifties, which a counsellor assured me was due to suppressed anger inside which had deepened and hardened over the years. (The 'Choice Theory' school of counselling has discovered a link between suppressed anger and heart disease.)

Apart from having caring, loving parents, I submit that we also need to feel secure in the wider world, especially during our time in school, free from bullying and free from fear of failure, which is so often induced by our pressurised system of education. Were the Ancient Greeks, who taught us so much, forced to sit stressful exams, on which so much is made to depend?

Sadly, we live in a fiercely competitive, self-seeking society, where we are all taught that personal achievement is all that matters, rather than love and respect for each other as well as ourselves. You may like to read my formula for a happier, healthier and well-ordered society, as enshrined in a letter I wrote to our Prime Minister last year, and also my latest letter to my local newspaper, the Bury Free Press, which I enclose herewith and which I hope will engage your interest.

Anatomy of a Society

The Royal College of Psychiatrists
16-11-11

I sincerely hope you will read the following with an open mind, as no offence is intended.

I am convinced from my own experience and from my conversations with others that suppressed anger is in most cases the root cause of clinical depression, which is so common in our society today. Perhaps I am stating something you already know and acknowledge, as a period of counselling often exposes the anger, just as it did with me. But counselling, as I believe, does not itself cure the problem, which requires an act of forgiveness before the anger and hatred inside can be removed for ever. In my case the ninth step of Alcoholics Anonymous, known as the 'amends' step, came to my rescue. I wrote a brief letter to my deceased father, whom I had hated for years, which went as follows: "Dear Dad, I'm sorry I always blamed you for everything that went wrong in my life and I hope you are happy and well in Heaven." It may defy belief, but in that moment I felt a huge burden was lifted. My anger evaporated. I felt re-born and since that time there has been no sign of the depression which previously blighted my life.

Counselling was part of my cure, but forgiveness was all-important in bringing about a full and successful recovery from what is in essence a spiritual illness. It is one thing to recognise the anger within, quite another to remove it entirely, and I would recommend the programme of Alcoholics Anonymous to anyone with serious emotional problems - not just to problem drinkers, who also frequently harbour deep-rooted resentments inside.

The Times
14-04-08

There must be so many current requests for public inquiries into corrupt or bad practice, that decades could pass before armies of lawyers and judges could carry them through - at huge cost to the state

Whatever happened to honesty and trust between members of our community in the UK? I can remember a time, soon after the war, when doors were left unlocked at night, you could leave your bike unattended, unchained in the street and the word 'mugging' had yet to be coined. We may be richer and even live longer than ever before, but how many people are happy? The frown on the faces of people I see in the street says it all.

Perhaps we should train children to care more for each other - love being the greatest healer of all.

Everest Double Glazing
Copy The Office of Fair Trading
Copy David Ruffley M
Copy Clare Short MP
23-03-09

NOTICE OF LEGAL PROCEEDINGS

In my absence, my wife, who is 65 and in failing health, welcomed into her home an accredited representative of your company to discuss a new set of windows and doors, which badly need replacing, with the strict instruction from myself for her not to sign up for a deal without my explicit consent. In the event, she was subjected to a gruelling ordeal for more than three hours to persuade her to sign there and then, which left her emotionally exhausted.

For my part, as part owner of the house, all I required was the best possible price for the job in writing, with details as specified by my wife and agreed with your representative, to be valid for three months and to be paid in full by myself and my wife on completion of the work to her satisfaction.

My personal view of the matter is that the work could be done for around six thousand pounds, a lot less than was quoted, which you can take or leave as you please, but my primary concern is to obtain a written apology from your company for the unnecessary and serious distress caused to my wife, which in my view amounts to harassment.

If my wife fails to receive an apology, I can assure you that I will know how to act.

To two valued AA friends

I hope you don't mind reading this little letter, which was only written because I have always had the greatest respect for you both.

Perhaps I am stating the obvious, but it seems to me that the amount people drink largely depends on their state of mind. Those who drink no more than the 'recommended' amount probably have such a measure of peace that they simply don't need to 'escape from themselves' by drinking much greater quantities of alcohol, or indeed any other palliative.

I know, of course, that practising alcoholics are full of resentments and fears, with no peace of mind at all, and that the craving for alcohol completely takes over their lives, as it did mine for many years, which is why the Fellowship of Alcoholics Anonymous has always maintained that the only way out of their misery is total abstinence for the rest of their lives.

Nonetheless, when I finally applied myself to the 12 steps of AA, all my anger and fears from the past were eventually taken away and replaced with feelings of love, and to my amazement, I later found I could drink without getting angry or drunk, just like most 'social' drinkers. Although I am aware of some measure of craving, because I am a regular drinker, I know when I've had 'enough', and when I have company I seldom think about drink at all

As you must have guessed, the whole time I spent in AA I was still full of resentments and fears. I hadn't even attempted a proper 3rd step, and like many others, all I did every day was to pray not to drink, which of course isn't the programme at all. The daily prayer which eventually led to my crucial 3rd step was as follows: "Dear Lord, please take care of my will and my life this day, because I cannot manage on my own!" - following which I began to get 'conscious contact' with God. (As you may imagine, I was pretty desperate at the time, having fallen hopelessly in love with a woman at work who was happily married with children, while I also was married with two fine sons, one of whom was very ill at that time.) My step 4 ran into page after page on computer and I've since written a whole book on the need for more love and more honesty in our self-seeking, soulless society today.

I still deeply regret the anguish I caused my family when I was a raging alcoholic, with one face for my family and another for the outside world, but I do have a measure of peace I have never known before, having found the love 'in me', which resides deep down in us all, and which is the greatest blessing I ever received in my life.

I did become very ill with a series of manic attacks after having a dreadful time when I was homeless, but I only picked up a drink again during my third or fourth manic attack, when I escaped from hospital and ended up in the buffet/bar on Kings Lynn railway station! (My son, Mathew, who is hugely better, and teases me all the time, says I must hold "the world record" for admissions to G8!) The truth is you wouldn't believe all the 'shit' I've been through since I handed my will and my life over to God, but I expect it will all turn out well in the end. At least I've withdrawn from an incredibly stressful relationship, while my wife, who used to be so dependent, has become a 'tower of strength' after having to cope on her own without me.

by Neville Lewis

Of course I would never recommend drinking again to any recovering alcoholic, but I thought you might like to hear some of my story, after I finally plucked up the courage to do my 3rd step, after which the rest of the steps followed in quick succession. I've repaid all my debts and have even saved enough money to pay for my funeral - which for a former spendthrift is no mean achievement (!), and although 'true love' has passed me by, I am happier now than at any time in my past.

Thanks for reading this letter, and I hope you are both keeping well,

Love and best wishes

The British Medical Association
26-02-08

Further to my letter of 21-02-08 regarding the freedom to smoke, perhaps I can elaborate on my belief that a great deal of illness is due to a 'lack of love' at some point in our lives, especially if we are starved of love during childhood.

I acknowledge that there are many who find the strength to rise above great adversity or the pain of an awful childhood through the expression of a particular talent, which gives their lives meaning and purpose and some sense of satisfaction. Others sometimes find love later in life, which gives them a feeling of well-being and freedom from mental illness or addiction to drink or drugs.

However, members of the Fellowship of Alcoholics Anonymous recognise that for them drink is just 'the tip of the iceberg' and that a whole range of resentments and fears from the past must be removed, before they can feel happy inside and free from their dreadful addiction. Many, of course, have also been mentally ill and or involved in violent behaviour, either at home or outside in the wider community, and we all know there is a world of difference between a 'happy drunk', who merely causes amusement, and an unruly drunk, whose anger erupts when he drinks.

It is, of course, only too easy to blame alcohol itself for the many problems it seems to bring, while completely ignoring the impact of deep-rooted feelings on health and behaviour. Perhaps my own experience of poor mental health and addiction to alcohol may help shed some light on the issue, and to that end I enclose a couple of extracts from my book entitled "The Truth About Love', which I regret has never been published.

Anatomy of a Society

The British Medical Journal
14-11-07

I am convinced that the amount people drink, eat or take drugs largely depends on their state of mind and that those who have anger, anxiety or guilt feelings inside are most likely to drink, eat or take drugs to excess for relief. I am certain a few simple questions would soon reveal the root cause of their problem, which may go right back, as mine did, to childhood, although the addict himself may be quite unaware of the impact of distant events in his life on his current behaviour.

Human beings are more than machines, and I submit that the huge pressures we place on our children today only serve to promote emotional stress and poor mental health or wayward behaviour in years to come, especially for those whose security has already been undermined by broken or disturbed homes. Thankfully, there are some who find love later in life, which totally changes their lives, as it did mine - love being the greatest healer of all.

Please find enclosed a copy of my recent letter to our Prime Minister and two extracts from a book which I wrote five years ago, which I hope you will find time to read.

The Bury Free Press
6-03-11

A female acquaintance recently told me that many of her friends would prefer to remain at home taking care of their families, but that the cost of housing forced them to go out to work. Females in general, or so I have found, have more warmth and compassion than males, who much prefer to be the breadwinners, which for most men is a matter of pride.

There are exceptions, of course, but it seems to me that females should be given sufficient financial support with housing to enable them stay at home and look after their families, if that is their preferred option, bearing in mind that their role in the home is just as important as that of their male counterparts in work. The grossly misnamed 'Sure Start' system of care, which encourages mothers of very young children to go out to work, is surely the opposite of what is needed, if both young and old are to receive the love and attention they need and deserve.

We all need lots of love during early life if we are to avoid a life of crime or anti-social behaviour, the risk of addiction to drink or drugs or the misery of mental illness - as I know from my own harsh experience of life.

by Neville Lewis

The Independent
10-9-11

As long as we encourage females, especially mothers of very young children, to go out to work, either through choice or necessity, in order to maximise GDP, I suggest we will continue to incur huge costs in terms of care for the young, the sick and the elderly, who in former times were cared for at home, at a time when most bread-winners were males, which for centuries was their natural role in society and still is in many parts of the world. How ironic it is that many thousands of females make a living caring for the children of others, while their own offspring are being cared for by their out-of-work husbands! Meanwhile their ageing parents are being dumped into homes for the elderly, at huge expense, in a society where at the same time a third of the population now live on their own, contrary to all that is natural to human beings, who are gregarious by nature and need the love of their families more than anything else to maintain their ongoing health and security.

The current high incidence of mental illness and anti-social behaviour is a measure of how our society has changed since I was a boy, when most females preferred to remain in the home taking care of their children and their elderly relatives, at far less cost to themselves or the economy, a woman's love being the rock on which any caring society is based - a love which is surely priceless!

The Guardian
7-12-11

I hate to denigrate the opposite sex, but where are the women of days gone by, who stuck by their man and stayed mainly at home to take care of their young and their elderly relatives? I have met many males in Bury who became homeless when their relationships failed due to their partners' infidelity, also a number of young men who became ill or disturbed after being abandoned by their own mothers when they moved on to another relationship. While some males clearly behave badly, I can recall a time when such behaviour in any female was widely condemned, yet in today's world it seems to be seen as perfectly acceptable. I have met several females in recent years who said they would sooner be at home taking care of their families, but that the high cost of housing forced them to remain in work. Who, nonetheless, can really believe them, when few women would wish to relinquish their independence, while every Friday and Saturday night one sees crowds of scantily-clad females scouring our streets, clubs and pubs in search of sex?

For me one of the saddest signs of the times was the recent appeal by the YMCA - in St Edmundsbury's publication, 'Community Spirit' - for volunteers in West Suffolk to take in homeless 16- and 17-year-olds on a temporary basis, who presumably come from homes short on love. I sincerely hope none of them dies from the winter cold before help can be found!

The Royal College of Psychiatrists
1-9-11

There is more to mental illness than meets the eye and it is often caused by a hopeless or desperate situation. While in hospital on various occasions, I met many patients who, like myself, had received powerful tranquillisers to calm their disturbed behaviour and who, for a variety of reasons, had failed to cope with their current situation.

Several had lost their jobs and had become morbidly anxious when they failed to get back into remunerative work, despite all their efforts. I felt particularly sorry for one man, who had been advised by his solicitor to throw in his job and to resort to social security, simply because he couldn't afford to maintain his four children after his marriage had failed. He clearly had valued his job and just couldn't face the prospect of such a grim future. Another man had waited so long for an eye operation, which he desperately needed to keep his job as a lorry driver that the anxiety became too much for him to bear and so he too became mentally ill. I also met a man who assured me he only became ill after pleading in vain many times for help from Social Services to assist him in taking care of his ailing parents, who needed more support than he could give on his own.

One poor woman clearly became ill because she found it impossible to cope financially, when she was obliged to live on state support, as she repeatedly and bitterly complained during her 'treatment'. Another had fallen ill following a long period of physical abuse from her disturbed son. There were other patients who clearly had deep-rooted problems arising from some kind of abuse in their past, some from one or both of their parents during their childhood, abuse which they could not forgive. There were also those who had lost a loved one, with no help or support with their grief. One poor woman I met was in a dreadful state, unable to utter a word to express her grief or to respond to a word of comfort. I also met several patients who sadly had become addicted to drugs and were struggling to beat their addiction, while others were clinically depressed after failing to cope with an adverse event in their lives or a deeply stressful situation, from which there seemed no escape.

by Neville Lewis

In my case, I only became mentally ill after suffering the horrors of homelessness when my relationship failed, thereafter no longer being capable of work, partly because of the debilitating side-effects of my 'medication'. I know several males in my locality who suffered precisely the same fate when their relationships failed and who are no longer able to work. (I understand nearly 40,000 homes in our country are currently being re-possessed every year and that the charity, Shelter, has forecast a huge increase in homelessness as the proposed 'cuts' begin to bite.)

Victims of mental illness surely need all the love and support we can give, both in terms of counselling to deal with the vexed feelings inside and as much help as is possible to address their particular needs. Too many by far are treated with ongoing 'medication', as if their condition is hopeless - medication which in itself often has a disabling effect on some patients, their emotional problems buried for years, along with their former vitality and zest for living! In a more caring, enlightened society, clearly much mental illness could be avoided, while with the right support at the right time many more victims could fully recover, thereby saving the state a fortune in ongoing care.

There is indeed much more to mental illness than meets the eye and its high incidence, undeserved stigma and sometimes deplorable treatment are symptoms of a society which seems to have lost its soul.

The British Medical Journal

Apart from disturbed or broken relationships, there are of course many other reasons for emotional stress leading to poor mental and physical health, including poverty. We know that the life expectancy of residents in deprived areas, where there are high levels of unemployment and crime, is much lower than in more affluent areas, suggesting a link between financial security and personal safety and health. I believe even sibling rivalry, arising from feelings of jealousy and resentment, sometimes when a second child arrives on the scene and the first-born receives less love and attention, can lead to emotional problems which run on for years.

But I believe huge social changes since the last war, particularly in the UK, have also contributed to an increase in levels of anxiety in large parts of the population, with an ongoing impact on health. When I was a young boy, just after the war, I believe there was much more trust within our society than there is now. At least in the town where I was born and raised, doors were left unlocked at night and a bicycle could safely be left in the street with no padlock or chain to secure it. I shall never forget being told by an aunt how shocked she was some years later, when a policeman came round and told her to keep her door locked as there were thieves in the area! Since the end of the war and the growth in the supply of luxury goods, greed for money and what it can buy has led to all kinds of fraud and deceit, as we all know, even such things as identity theft and the cloning of cash cards, which we all fear could happen to us. Meanwhile, all doors remain locked at all times, bicycles need padlocks and chains to protect them from theft and many premises are fitted with burglar alarms - which shows how insecure people must now feel with respect to their property.

Another major change since the end of the war has been the shift in the role of many mothers of young children, who currently, through choice or necessity, divide their time between working and taking care of their families, which must cause considerable strain on their mental and emotional resources, as well as their children's emotional security. The second half of the 20th century also saw an end to the stigma surrounding divorce and a huge increase in casual or broken relationships. As a result, a third of the population now live on their own, some finding it difficult to cope with the loneliness of their situation, in a society which has become more an assemblage of self-seeking individuals than the close-knit community I knew as a boy, which was based on old-fashioned family love and the need to share scarce resources, especially food, after the ravages of war had left the country virtually broke. Because of their need for each other, I believe most people were truthfully happier than they are now and I suspect as a result there was less incidence of mental illness, although I expect there are no statistics available to prove my point.

Finally, another source of acute emotional stress is our increasingly pressurised system of education, with its obsession with standards of performance and its close scrutiny of every child's progress and the ability of teachers to teach. There also seems an assumption that learning is simply a tool to improve the economy and to enable our young to obtain a 'successful' career. When I was a boy there were no league tables for schools and far fewer pupils expected to go on to higher education. There were no tuition fees and a generous grant was provided to cover the cost of accommodation and keep while at university. In my view, the huge number of young people who are now persuaded to aspire to a university education is disproportionate to the need and leads to the alarming prospect, which many now face, of being hugely in debt before even starting a job.

I am convinced that the social changes I have described all contribute to emotional stress and it is therefore hardly surprising that one in four of the population now become mentally ill at some stage in their lives. As for the growing threat of obesity and its impact on health, I can only recall one boy in my class who could not climb a rope in the gymnasium because of his weight. Such foods as fried chips, chocolate and crisps were just as available then, as now, so it seems to me that it must be emotional stress which causes many children to binge on fatty foods for comfort from stress in the current climate.

As for the need for less greed and more love in our society today, I may seem naive, but it seems to me that only the power of true love, which has been celebrated in song, story and verse throughout the ages, has the potential to bring social change which would benefit health and everyone's quality of life. I see love, especially the love of a mother, as being essential to the health and well being of any child and if necessary we should encourage such love with sufficient financial support to sustain it whenever the will and the desire of the mother is clear. Meanwhile some mothers even leave their children behind when they move on to another relationship and I have met a number of young males who became mentally ill following such an event in their lives.

With regard to my own experience of mental illness, I suffered a severe attack of anxiety and depression when I was 21, which ended my university career. It was only many years later that with great pain and much love and support from a woman with whom I worked, I withdrew from my medication and with the help of counselling, as memories came flooding back, I discovered my problem was suppressed anger at the way my father treated my mother when I was a child. I then came to realise my poor father was badly affected by the war. The moment I forgave the past, feelings of anger and fear were replaced by feelings of love, the love which, as I believe, resides deep down in us all.. I felt a huge burden was lifted and at once I found peace and new hope and strength for the future, a change I shall never forget.

Such is the enduring power of love in all of our lives, if we can only manage to find it!

29-3-11
Dear Mr Humphrys.

I was particularly interested to hear today's programme, 'On the Ropes', in which you interviewed Adam Ant. When I became ill after a long spell of homelessness, I too was diagnosed with bi-polar disorder.and I sincerely hope you will find time to read the enclosed extracts from my book, 'A Place to Stay', which highlight some of the treatment which I received.

In my experience, it is extremely difficult to withdraw from major tranquillisers and anti-depressants without the support of counselling, while such drugs only tend to bury the problem, which means the patient, in many cases, has no access to the vexed feelings inside and therefore no hope of a cure. For that reason alone, many medical practitioners seem to believe that bi-polar disorder is incurable, which is simply not the case, because it is due to emotional stress, which can be addressed and removed.

The Mental Health Alliance
19-06-07

I submit it is simply not possible for Central Government to ensure that any new guidelines for the treatment of mental illness, however well-intended, are followed to the letter by each individual clinician or health worker across the country, all of whom can be completely mistaken in their assessment of risk to the patient or the community.

For that reason, I am passionately opposed to any legislation which gives the power to any clinician or health worker to force vulnerable people to take medication they may NOT need, once they are out of section. The power, in addition, to confine some in their homes, I find quite appalling and frightening, knowing myself how distressing and stressful the loss of one's freedom can be!

Dr Harcourt
27-10-07

Please find enclosed a copy of my latest 'care plan'. My thoughts about 'early warning signs' are as follows.

I only "over-react" when the truth is denied or when I am stressed through lack of sleep, as any healthy, normal man does. (I find it extremely annoying that my psychiatrists have consistently denied the truth that my medication affects the circulation in my legs - a fact which I know to be true).

It also says in my care plan that " he can also become anxious when stressed and worried about his finances." I submit it is perfectly normal for a person who is 2000 pounds in debt to the bank and has no money to pay for accommodation and cannot obtain further credit, to be somewhat concerned by his situation - even more so if he is eventually forced to face the dreadful prospect of cold winter nights out in the open and possibly death from hypothermia.

I have since repaid all my debts, so I have no further worries over my finances. I also have a nice comfortable home and a warm bed and plenty of money for heating during the winter months, so my situation has hugely improved since I first became ill when I was homeless. If I could have obtained accommodation of any kind at the start when I first found myself homeless, I could have got quickly back into work and saved the state a fortune in health care costs.

Thanks for reading this letter.

To Dr Mayhew
Copy My CPN
18-09-08

I hope you get to read this letter before my review next Monday.

In my experience, most mental illness appears to be due to acute anxiety and anger because one's basic needs for love and security are threatened or not being met. In my case, the main cause of my illness was having been homeless for four miserable months, when I not only lost a great deal of sleep, but also became fearful I might not survive the winter and very angry that nobody seemed to care! Also, those I have since met who have worked with the homeless all say that it takes a full year to recover for every month spent 'sleeping rough' on the street. As you must know, my situation has long since changed and I've had a warm bed and a roof over my head for a number of years. My finances are also in good order and I've repaid all my debts, so the anger and fear that I had when I was homeless have all gone away.

As you know, I was vexed and unhappy with Dr Grover's assessment and it seems that you have the same myopic view as he did. I can assure you that it is possible to withdraw successfully from anti-psychotic drugs, in spite of the fact that the withdrawals can be quite stressful. That is something I fully accept, but I must be free from my medication if I am to have an acceptable quality of life in my declining years, simply because the side-effects of Chlopixol are so severe. I therefore wish to switch from injections to tablets, the level of which I can reduce very slowly at my discretion until I am free from withdrawals altogether and have a far better quality of life.

Please find attached my perceived list of side-effects, which comes from a book which I wrote six years ago, entitled 'The Truth About Love'. The main reason I quit my job and left my wife at the same time was because I wasn't getting enough love. I could give you details, but I doubt you would believe my story, nor why I was homeless for such a long time. After all, your remit is just to treat symptoms, not to delve into causes.

Sorry to be such a pain!

The Bury Free Press
27-4-07

I would just like to thank the health authorities who recommended the drug known as Clopixol for people like me, who became ill after being homeless and losing a great deal of sleep 'sleeping rough' and exposed to the elements..

Quite by accident, my CPN, who administers the drug every four weeks, made my latest appointment for five weeks instead of four. After four weeks and a few days I became very stressed with the withdrawals from the drug. I even began being irritable at times with my family, and as my CPN said, I must not get irritable, however stressed I may feel. Anyway, thanks to my recent injection, I've had a good sleep and am nice and amenable and docile again, and able to take any abuse without getting angry. Meanwhile, the state saves a great deal of money, keeping me well sedated and out of hospital.

I don't mind too much being 'a zombie', but of course I am tired and lethargic for most of the time and sadly I cannot appreciate music as much as I used to because of the medication, which buries most of my feelings and most of the confidence I used to have in myself. Nonetheless, I do still get pleasure, like any other animal, I guess, from eating, sleeping and defecating, and I do at least have a home which protects me from the cold, the wind and the rain and a nice warm bed instead of the cold, hard pavement - for which I am truly grateful. I have several friends who receive similar 'treatment', all of whom became homeless - mainly through failed relationships - before they became ill, and all of whom have been classified as 'disabled', perhaps from the effects of their ongoing 'medication'?

Sometimes I wonder if any doctor or nurse would have the courage to take the same medicine for a few months - just to discover how hard it can be to recover - but somehow I doubt there would be any volunteers! Thankfully, most women have first claim on the home when relationships fail, which empowers them to do as they please with their partners. I guess that explains why I have never seen any females toting 'The Big Issue' in Bury.

by Neville Lewis

The Royal College of Psychiatrists
30-04-08

Psychiatrists call it 'medication', but I prefer the term 'desecration'!

I refer, of course, to such anti-psychotic drugs as Chlorpromazine, Stelazine or Chlopixol, which while keeping me 'sane', did bury my feelings for many years and left me with little appreciation of the finer things of life, such as music, poetry, painting and, more especially, love.

However, I did have two really good years free from drugs after falling in love at the age of 56 - love being the greatest healer of all. Although my love failed and I became ill once again after having been homeless for several months, I can honestly say, in the words of Shelley, the poet, "it is better to have loved and lost than never to have loved at all!"

Indeed, it was love which gave me the power to understand and forgive my poor father, whom I had hated for years, and which gave me a measure of peace which I know I shall have for the rest of my time on earth, having found the love "in me" which, despite all "the slings and arrows of outrageous fortune", resides deep down in us all.

The Chief Executive
NICE
18-04-08

How would you like to be neither happy nor sad for years at a time, your only pleasures being eating, sleeping and defecating and the only motive that drives you the will to survive?

If you would like to enjoy such a blissfully sterile existence, try taking one of your excellent drugs, namely Chlopixol, which I presume you recommend for the treatment of bi-polar effective disorder, with which I was diagnosed 10 years ago after having been homeless for four terrible months following the breakdown of a relationship.

My psychiatrist says that Chlopixol is not habit-forming. Perhaps one of your staff could try it sometime - and then see if he can successfully withdraw from the stuff without going crazy!

Anatomy of a Society

MHRA
24-03-08
Copy Dr Harcourt

I have to say I thought your Yellow Card was badly worded and sometimes ridiculous. How can anyone report his own death, for goodness sake? Even the return freepost envelope couldn't be sealed, so I had to make do with strips of sellotape.

As a mental health patient, although I loathe cooking, at least I can boil an egg and heat up a few beans out of a tin, but I'm damned if I could make sense of your card, which I could scarcely read even with glasses.

Why not simply ask for the presumed side-effects of the medication and leave it at that?

The Royal College of Psychiatrists
5-12-11

I cannot thank my regime of treatment enough for wrecking my quality of life for the past 14 years after I suffered a painful, stress-related illness following a long and unexpected spell of homelessness. Mercifully, the drugs I was given, which are widely prescribed by members of your profession, destroyed any hope I might have had of returning to work, thanks to their beautifully vicious, distressing side-effects.

However, with much sorrow, I have to report that despite all the efforts of your colleagues, I am now virtually free from such lovely drugs after a long and painful withdrawal on my own stupid initiative. I am so grateful the drugs concerned, with their curdling effect on the brain, reduced me to a walking zombie for so many years. It is indeed sad and regrettable that I now have a new lease of life and enjoy living again, despite the kind help and advice I have been given by members of your fraternity over the years.

The Guardian
6-9-11

After a lifetime in work, I suddenly found myself homeless, at the age of 58, with no money to pay for accommodation, following the breakdown of my relationship. After four terrible months 'sleeping rough' on the street, I suffered a series of manic

by Neville Lewis

attacks, for which I was hospitalised, at great cost to the NHS, for months at a time. Partly due to the side-effects of my 'medication' and the lack of job opportunities, I was no longer able to get back into work. Since that time I have become acquainted with several males in my own locality, all capable men, who became homeless and then mentally ill for the same reason and no longer capable of work as a result. It is worth mentioning that males of working age who become homeless are not considered 'priority' for housing by local councils, and as a result many become 'trapped' for years in the same situation, languishing for long periods in crowded night shelters or hostels for the homeless, with little chance of escape back to the comfortable world they once knew - unless they fall ill, as I did, and have to remain in hospital or a 'care home', at huge cost to the tax-payer, until a subsidised home eventually becomes available from the local authority's limited housing stock. In my case, I reckon the cost of my care would have covered the cost of the rent on my flat for a good many years!

Apart from broken relationships, there are, of course, other reasons why people become homeless. Currently, 40,000 homes are being re-possessed every year across the UK and the charity, Shelter, has forecast a major increase in homelessness as the proposed cuts begin to bite. Meanwhile, little is said about the potentially huge cost to the NHS, as many more, no doubt, become mentally ill and disabled for life as a result of losing their homes - a home being essential to the health and indeed survival of all human beings.

How sad it is that little thought is given to the underlying cost of homelessness, both in terms of money and suffering, at a time when a million homes are currently standing empty in the UK. I have sent copies of this letter to those in charge of our health, but no doubt all they will do is pass on my letter to the people responsible for housing, a different department of government which has no remit regarding matters of health and therefore will not see why it should or how it can help, given its own limited budget!

The Bury Free Press
29-11-06

I was somewhat surprised when I saw the recent BBC programme on homelessness, which involved several people addicted to drink or drugs. In my case, like many others, I had always lived close to the limit of credit allowed by my bank, but I was totally free from any addiction, when unexpectedly I found myself 'skint', with no home to go to. Sadly, I'd fallen hopelessly in love with a woman at work, who failed to respond and stayed loyal and true to her husband. As a result, I eventually quit my job and left my poor wife and fled broken-hearted to Scotland, where I had recently been on a walking holiday.

On my return, I found, understandably, that I was no longer welcome in the marital home. I applied for work, but was told I must wait eight days before I could get any money, which was too late for my needs. I then applied to the DSS for a crisis loan, but was referred instead to the old Lathbury centre in Bury, where I was turned away when it opened at six because it was full. I then applied for a loan, to be guaranteed by my share of the equity in the marital home, but was refused because I was no longer in work.

In desperation, I turned to my doctor, who saw how agitated I was (after 48 hours with no sleep), and gave me a sick note. He also referred me to a psychiatrist, who asked if I had "special powers", as I stood before her with empty pockets and nowhere to stay! She could find nothing wrong - except that I had no money on which to live!

In the end, I scrounged ten pounds from my poor wife and in anger hitched all the way back to Scotland, living on bread and jam, chocolate and orange squash and sleeping in bus shelters, shop doorways and once under the arch of a bridge which spanned a river. - until my benefit came through. There is much more I could tell, but suffice to say, after four months or so tramping the streets back in England in search of accommodation, I became more and more disorientated through lack of sleep and fell ill with a series of manic attacks, which knocked me for six and put an end to all hope of getting back into work.

I am grateful for all the help I have since received from my carers and local council over the years, but I reckon if I'd received the support at the start to supply all my needs, I could have got back into work and saved the state enough money to purchase my council flat outright.

The Bury Free Press
1-01-10

Homelessness can happen to anyone. It frequently happens when a relationship fails or when a person loses his job and cannot keep up with the mortgage or rent on his home. Whatever the cause, a person is effectively homeless when he has no money to pay for accommodation and no-one will take him in.

by Neville Lewis

I believe it was Margaret Thatcher who made benefit payable in arrears, out of step with the need, and in my case I had to wait a fortnight before I received the statutory allowance after making my claim. With just ten pounds in my pocket, which was all I had to my name, and because the home for the homeless in Bury was full, I somehow survived on bread and jam, chocolate and orange squash, sleeping in shop doorways, bus shelters and once under the arch of a bridge which spanned a river, until my benefit came through - thankfully without having to beg or to turn to crime to survive. I was lucky that it was summer when I first became homeless and I also had a sleeping bag, but I shudder to think how anyone will cope who is made homeless in Bury this winter if all the places for homeless people are full. Indeed, the main priority seems to be to make our town a paradise for shoppers, with adverts for the 'Arc' even appearing on the Tube in London! Surely, as a community, we also have a duty of care for those less fortunate, especially anyone who is found 'sleeping rough' and whose life is seriously at risk at this time of year.

In most towns there is plenty of private accommodation, but since the law changed and housing benefit is no longer paid direct to the landlord, but instead to the prospective tenant, most private landlords insist that their tenants must be in work, which is hard to obtain when one is 'sleeping rough' with no fixed address - not to mention the stigma attached to the homeless!

In my case I eventually fell ill due to the stress of the situation and could no longer work - the irony being that my ongoing treatment and care has cost the taxpayer an arm and a leg ever since - much more than it would have cost Bury Council to find me a place to stay for a few weeks until I got back on my feet and back into work. I also know from people I've met that my case is not unique.

The Rt Hon Nick Clegg
Deputy Prime Minister
10-06-10

There are thousands of people in our society whose homes are currently being repossessed when they have lost their jobs and have thereby been made homeless, although in my case I became homeless after my marriage broke down and I became mentally ill after being 'stranded' on 'the street' for several months.

For anyone in such a situation there is little hope of finding another job in the current climate, especially if one is 'sleeping rough' with no fixed address. I also have it on good authority that for every month living from hand to mouth on 'the street' it takes a year to recover. I am sure this is true, because I was in and out of hospital a number of times, at great cost to the NHS and Social Services, before my health stabilised - and sadly by that time I had reached the end of my working life and was due to retire. Looking back, I reckon the money it cost the NHS for my care and the cost to my local council in terms of housing and council tax benefit would have purchased the flat outright which I now rent and which was eventually provided by my Council. I understand there are currently 1700 families on my Council's waiting list for affordable housing, while the annual supply of social housing is just a fraction of what is required.

If we wish to save future costs arising from the problem of homelessness, I would urgently stress the need for more social housing and an end to the right to buy at a discount for tenants, a policy which has seriously depleted the stock of social housing in recent years. A roof over one's head is vital to a person's survival, so surely the provision of social housing should be a top priority for any Council and any Government.

Of course, there are hostels and night shelters for the homeless in various towns, but I suggest that you visit Jimmy's night shelter in Cambridge for a taste of what being homeless is really like and what it does to the human psyche. If nothing has changed, I suspect you will be shocked - just as I was when I was one of their clients!

The British Medical Association
Copy 'Shelter'
Copy The Minister for Housing
Copy The Health Protection Agency
29-02-08

I cannot understand how anyone can set a figure on the number of unfortunate people 'sleeping rough' at any one time in England or the UK. When I was homeless, I was constantly moving from town to town, often on foot, in my desperate search for permanent accommodation. When money allowed, I used to stay the odd night in Youth Hostels, cheek by jowl with hikers and ramblers, where no-one would have suspected that I was homeless. Like many others, I tried to remain as inconspicuous as possible, knowing full well that there is a stigma attached to the homeless, while pride and prudent management of my meagre resources prevented me from begging for money to live.

After several months I was lucky enough (?) to fall ill with a series of manic attacks due to the stress of my situation, and was given the luxury of a hospital bed and hot meals before the cold weather could finish me off. (I had been told that several

by Neville Lewis

homeless people had died on the streets of Cambridge during a cold snap near Christmas a few years earlier.) Please find enclosed an extract from my book, 'The Truth About Love', which highlights the problems I faced at that time.

Had I received help and support from the start when it was needed - enough at least so I could catch up with my sleep and then continue in work in my chosen profession, which was accounts, until my retirement date seven years on. - my quality of life would not have been wrecked and the state would have been spared a fortune in hospital costs and ongoing medical treatment. Unfortunately, housing benefit was only paid in arrears and then only after a place had been secured by a substantial deposit up front, which I just couldn't raise at the time.

I have several friends who also became mentally ill after having been homeless.

The Times
1-12-08

If more of our high-flying females in parliament had caring hearts, I am sure they would soon force a change in the law so that newcomers to 'the street' were given a warm bed and a roof over their head with immediate effect, in line with the law in Scotland. When I was homeless in Cambridge, I was horrified to learn that a number of homeless people had previously died from the cold on the city's illustrious streets, during a cold snap near Christmas a few years ago.

With so many home repossessions currently taking place, I shudder to think what the death toll for our homeless may be in glorious England this winter.

The Bury Free Press
27-08-07

Following the farce over a giro, which I described in my earlier letter, I realise in hindsight that I was effectively 'trapped' on the street by 'the system', as there was no way I could find the money to pay a deposit up front on a place and I just couldn't afford bed and breakfast accommodation or lodgings. I did eventually manage to find a job selling newspapers at a roadside kiosk in Cambridge, but I was still 'sleeping rough' at the time and autumn frosts were beginning to bite. Soon after acquiring the job, I began to fall ill through lack of sleep and exhaustion, which as you know led to a series of manic attacks, for which it seems I shall need treatment for the rest of my life, in spite of the crippling side-effects of my medication. Perhaps Margaret Thatcher someday will realise how cruel and counter-productive it was to try to stop any abuse of the benefits system by denying support at the start when it is needed. As one of my sons jokingly says, "you've got to kick a man when he's down!" - but what is the point if the means are not there for a man to get back on his feet? As I said to the girls at the housing department in Haverhill, "I'm not a felon, but a respectable man down on his luck, who simply needs somewhere to live."

Unfortunately, I'd fallen in love with a woman at work, who sadly couldn't return my love because she was happily married with children, which is why I eventually quit my job and withdrew from a very unhappy marriage at the same time. I had applied to an agency in Bury for a new job in accounts, but I never imagined for a moment, after many years in full-time employment, that it would be so difficult to get back into work or to find a new home once I was homeless, nor that all the resources and courage I had, at the age of fifty-eight, would become focussed on a grim battle just to survive!

Gordon Brown MP
Prime Minister
24-11-08

After a night in the open in the freezing cold without any sleep, I can assure you from personal experience that it is simply not possible to follow the requisite procedures to obtain a warm bed and a roof over one's head, which currently involves securing a place to stay with a substantial deposit and rent up front before housing benefit is approved and granted by the local housing authority.

In view of the current number of repossessions due to the financial crisis, please please can we go back to the system where private landlords were happy to take on anyone who found himself destitute and homeless, when rent was paid direct by the local Council to the landlord concerned as soon as the need arose? After all, the claimant's credentials can soon be established a day or two after the person concerned has been housed and saved from the cold.

In my case I was obliged to spend several months 'sleeping rough' and as a result I became very ill, since which time I have cost the state a great deal, not only in terms of ongoing treatment, but also in terms of incapacity benefit and Housing and Council Tax benefit over a period of ten years until the date of my retirement.

As the saying goes, "a stitch in time saves nine" - not only in terms of money, but also in terms of lives. In hindsight I consider myself lucky to still be alive!

The Times

by Neville Lewis

30-10-09

Homelessness tends to carry a stigma, with the widespread suspicion that people in such a plight are either scroungers who don't wish to work or simply people who cannot manage their own affairs. Many bankers have also shown that they too cannot manage their own 'affairs', and it was their gross incompetence which led to the current recession and the surge in numbers of hard-working people losing their jobs and their homes.

The cruel irony is that bailed-out bankers can continue to pay themselves massive bonuses, while those they made homeless may never find work again, in part because of the stigma attached to the homeless!

Where, I ask, is the justice in that?

The Bury Free Press
11-05-08

Since females gained their independence, they no longer depend on their male partners for the means to live - and quite rightly so.

However, they usually have priority over the home when relationships fail and are free to 'sleep around' with impunity without losing the roof over their heads. As a result, 90% of our homeless are males, many of whom have been ejected on to the street when their partners 'moved on' to another relationship

Surely equal rights for the sexes, which females fought for years, should also apply to our males, many of whom become homeless through no fault of their own.

The Bury Free Press
14-07-09

When a woman 'moves on' to another relationship, as many do, she usually retains the family home, while her luckless partner, and sometimes even her male children who cannot 'get on' with their new 'father', are forced to fend for themselves on 'the street' or at best to live in temporary accommodation.

As a direct result, 90% of our homeless are males, often having to 'sleep rough' if they haven't the money to pay the deposit and rent up front on a place in the private sector, bearing in mind the lack of sufficient social housing to deal with the current need.

At a time when females are constantly campaigning for such things as equal pay and more places in parliament, surely males should have the same rights as females where housing is concerned, bearing in mind that the law quite rightly no longer allocates blame when relationships fail.

While I could never wish my worst enemy to suffer the trauma of having to 'sleep rough', maybe for months at a time, I cannot see any reason why females should blithely pass from one relationship to another without ever having to suffer the same.

The Bury Free Press
15-12-11

I hope you agree that a home is probably the most important necessity for any human being, yet currently it is the least affordable and the greatest burden on everyone's budget in our society today. I suggest there are two main reasons why such a situation prevails - firstly the fact that so many females are now out at work, when previously most would be at home taking care of their partners in work, their young and their ageing relatives, and secondly the fact that our banks have long since been making a killing from interest on mortgages, which virtually doubles the cost of a home.

Until we see a change in the hearts of the more caring sex and the role of our greed-driven banks, which feed so rapaciously on tax-payers' incomes, I see no end to the grave situation regarding the cost of a home. Meanwhile it grieves me to hear that the YMCA should be appealing, in St Edmundsbury's news letter, 'Community Spirit', for volunteers to take in homeless 16 and 17-year-olds on a temporary basis - which is a tragic reminder of the state of relationships and the general 'lack of love' in our society today. Surely change must come soon, before more people end up homeless or living alone than ever before in our history!

The Bury Free Press
28-10-09

I noted with some misgiving the statement in the autumn issue of 'Community Spirit' that "if you are homeless or threatened with losing your home the council may have a duty to provide you with temporary or permanent housing" - with the clear implication that some poor devils - even our own countrymen - will fail to be housed!
A home, however basic, is vital to life, especially in winter, so if we value human

life, as we claim to do, surely every council has a duty at least to house every person born and bred in our country who becomes homeless, with no exceptions, as is the case in Scotland.

The Bury Free Press
30-05-08

Having experienced the horrors of homelessness and the impact it has on one's health, I would like to express my gratitude to the Havebury Housing Partnership and Bury Council for providing me with a beautiful flat at an affordable rent.
I just wish there was more social housing, especially in places like Bury St Edmunds, where many young people can barely afford any kind of accommodation in the private sector, neither to rent or to buy.

I see a home as a necessity, rather than an investment, which, after all, we cannot take with us when we die!

To Smoke or Not to Smoke?

To NICE
3.06.06

There was a time when most people smoked cigarettes and died when quite young. I know a man who has smoked for seventy years and is only 83 and clearly at risk of premature death, while my mother, who suffered from passive smoking for years, only lived to be 91.

It is said that 106,000 people die from smoking each year in the UK, while the remaining 600,000 deaths are due to some other cause or causes unknown.

Thank God we know it's the smoking, not the stress, which causes ill health and premature death - consistent with the good fortune and happy childhood we all have in life...

Anatomy of a Society

To NICE
7.06.06

The fact that many smokers and passive smokers live to a grand old age seems to contradict all the assumptions about smoking and health. I still believe that the main cause of illness and premature death in many who smoke, as well as in many who don't, is emotional stress. The respiratory system especially seems easily weakened by stress, and I believe that anger and fear place great strain on the lungs and the heart. Why else did "sharp peaks in mortality rates for respiratory and infectious diseases" occur during the course of the First World War, and why else did a counsellor ascribe my own heart attack some years ago to suppressed anger inside?

I suspect that our lungs have first to be damaged by stress before they become blackened by cigarette smoke and premature death takes place, and I can see no other reason than that why so many smokers live on to a ripe old age. Some people, of course, are more robust than others, and can absorb the stresses and strains of everyday life and therefore continue to smoke with impunity. But more importantly, as far as our general health is concerned, I am convinced that a great deal depends on how well we are loved and how secure we feel, especially during our formative years, which tend to dictate how well we adjust and relate with others in later life.

There may not be much we can do about stress without changing the way we live as a society, but before we begin, we could at least acknowledge the truth that emotional stress plays havoc with people's health and that health and happiness are closely interlinked.

To NICE
12-05-07

When I was homeless, I was consumed with anger and fear that I might not survive the winter frosts. I was also physically exhausted and hugely stressed through lack of sleep. In the end, I returned to the marital home, where I had been so unhappy, and suffered my first manic attack. By the time I reached hospital, the attack was over and I was simply relieved to have a hot meal and a warm bed after months in the open, living from hand to mouth and constantly searching in vain for affordable accommodation.

The next day after admission, I was forced to take medication I didn't need, which effectively destroyed any real chance of a full and happy recovery from the ordeal I'd been through on 'the street'. My following manic attacks only occurred when I tried to withdraw from the medication I didn't need. Sadly, anti-psychotic drugs, once applied, take over the functions of the brain and leave the unfortunate victim to live the life of the living dead, with few feelings or responses - which has been my fate for the past nine years, since I was homeless and first became ill.

I nearly died from the cold when I was out on 'the street', and because of the 'treatment' I have since received, I have returned to smoking and drinking. I am sixty-seven years old, and frankly I don't give a damn if I am denied medical help with any ailment which may afflict me before I die, because of the fact that I smoke. There are plenty of pills in Boots to relieve any pain and plenty enough to bring it all to an end!

To NICE
1-06-07

Most accidents on our roads are acknowledged to be due to human error, but there are a multitude of reasons behind errors of judgement while driving. Alcohol consumption, of course, is a glaring example, as is the use of a mobile phone while driving. But there are other reasons, especially emotional stress.

Perhaps we are fearful of being late for work or for an important appointment, so we drive too fast for the conditions. Perhaps we have just learned that our partner has been unfaithful, and we are deeply disturbed and upset. Perhaps we have just had a row with our neighbour over a boundary fence, or one of our children has just fallen ill. Perhaps we've lost sleep after a row with our boss the previous day, or are worried about some other problem at work which it seems can't be resolved. Perhaps we've just lost a great deal of money through gambling, or run out of credit with the bank! The list of things which can affect our driving is endless.

Statistics suggest that tobacco smoke causes ill health and premature death, I prefer to believe it's emotional stress which is the more likely culprit, not only for those who smoke, but also for those who don't. Despite our great wealth as a nation, I see the UK as a 'failed' state, with virtually no love between its members, at any level or corner of our spiritually dead society.

The 'All in the Mind' Programme
BBC Radio 4
24-01-07

I listened to some of your programme last night, but switched off in disgust when all the wrong reasons were given to deny the comfort of smoking for those who are mentally ill. Mental illness is incredibly stressful. I should know, because it happened to me, and I can assure you that to recover from such acute stress and to withdraw from tobacco at the same time would have been quite unbearable for me, and would have posed a major obstacle to recovery from my illness.

I would also like to inform the programme that three people with whom I am acquainted became chronic asthmatics as soon as they gave up the habit! Another man in the mental ward I was in actually died of an asthma attack after assuring me he had never suffered from asthma before he was admitted to hospital and lost his freedom. Finally, my own father died in hospital from an asthma attack soon after his GP persuaded him to stop smoking.

Meanwhile, it may be of interest for you to know that my mother had six sons, all of whom smoked, as well as my father, yet she lived to be 91. How long does the programme think she would have lived if she hadn't been a passive smoker for many years? I also know a man who smoked for sixty years with no ill effects at all, and another who has been a smoker for seventy years. The former is now deceased, but as far as I know the latter is still hale and hearty as ever. Perhaps you can explain why they didn't both die in their 30's, 40's or 50's, as one might expect from all the statistics on smoking, also why I myself am still alive at the age of 67, after being a heavy smoker for more than 40 years.

With respect, I would be grateful to receive your wisdom and comments on the above.

The Health Protection Agency
30-01-07

I am relieved that our statisticians are at last waking up to the possibility that emotional stress is the chief cause of ill health in developed societies. I understand that a recent survey has come to the conclusion that it is stress in the mother, perhaps rather than smoking (?), which appears to cause harm to the unborn child.

by Neville Lewis

Doctors all know that when patients have blood pressure tests, anxiety sometimes affects the results, which surely suggests our emotional responses can easily influence our blood pressure levels and therefore our general health and well-being.

In fact, all the evidence which points to the morbid effects of smoking could just as easily apply to an excess of emotional stress, which surveys have shown is often linked to financial insecurity, broken or failing relationships, high levels of crime in the locality where one lives, and more especially a serious 'lack of love' during early childhood.

For me, the most obvious evidence that stress, although often accompanied by smoking or other addictions, is the real killer, is simply the fact that most serious illness occurs late in life, while one would surely expect all smokers, who mostly start smoking during their teens, to die in their thirties, forties or fifties - yet some people smoke for fifty, sixty or even seventy years, with no ill effects at all! Surely, it must be the daily pressure of living, which affects some more than others, that takes its toll and eventually kills us all - the sooner the more stressed we are.

I am convinced if at least we reduced the pressures we put on our young, which sometimes raise stress to unbearable levels, many more children would stay sickness-free and live happier, healthier lives in adulthood.

To NICE
19-05-07

Life is uncertain and makes many demands at the best of times, so it is hardly surprising that many people seek comfort from smoking and drinking in moderate amounts. However, it does seem that excessive levels of stress often lead to an escalation in such behaviour, which appears to have morbid effects on our health. Our lungs are especially sensitive to emotional stress, as is exemplified by such things as hyper-ventilation, stress-related asthma and the fact that "sharp peaks in mortality rates for respiratory and infectious diseases" occurred during the course of the First World War - presumably as news of the terrible slaughter of loved ones came through. It is surely also significant that most serious illness occurs late in life, as vital organs begin to fail after a lifetime of constant use.

The phenomenon of craving can be very stressful, especially where smoking is concerned, as the euphoric feeling induced by inhaling tobacco smoke is short-lived and the craving soon returns. It takes time to recover from stress, so the fact that the risk of having lung cancer recedes more and more over time after quitting the habit, seems to suggest it is stress, rather than smoking, which lies at the heart of the problem. I once met a retired car salesman, who said it took seven years to recover from the stress of his job!

The fact that the more people smoke the more likely they are to fall ill with lung cancer is also consistent with the suggestion that stress is the real killer, rather than smoking. I know a man who used to smoke two ounces of tobacco per day, who tells me the craving was dreadful. The same person says that before he quit smoking and drinking he tried a number of times to take his own life. Although I too have been mentally ill, with "bipolar effective disorder", which led me to smoke and to drink after a long period of abstinence, in my case the stress has been less, which is why I smoke less than an ounce every day and have never been tempted to take my own life. Moreover, a few years ago, tests revealed that my cholesterol level was close to normal, while that of my friend was dangerously high. Nonetheless, I have noticed whenever I come under pressure and become angry or anxious, I tend to smoke and to drink more than usual, until the pressure subsides and the problem has gone. So once again it does seem that emotional stress is a significant factor in determining how much one smokes, and that stress, rather than smoking itself, may be the root cause of some cancers and many other diseases.

On the same theme, it is surely worth noting that the risk of contracting lung cancer, and the failure rate for recovery from all types of cancer, is much greater than the national average in deprived parts of the UK, where there are high levels of unemployment and crime. I understand that on some housing estates people live in constant fear of being mugged or having their homes burgled. People on low income, or whose jobs are insecure, also tend to smoke more than those who have higher incomes and whose jobs are more secure, but I suggest it is the anxiety and fear which accompanies financial hardship and insecurity which is the real reason behind the statistics on smoking and health.

Health scares themselves tend to generate anxiety and fear, so those who don't smoke, but are exposed to cigarette smoke, perhaps by their partner in life, may well fear for their own health, as well as that of their spouse, and become more and more stressed - hence the statistics suggesting that 'passive smoking' is harmful to health.

Finally, as I have stated before, some men are more robust than others, and smoke for many years with no ill effects at all, while females, who have much greater emotional strength than most males, tend to live longer than men, which by my simple logic confirms it is stress which is the root cause of ill health among smokers - and most other people besides.

by Neville Lewis

House of Swan
Sword House
Totteridge Road
High Wycombe
HP13 6EJ
26.05.06

I am a happy smoker who rolls his own cigarettes, usually using Swan cigarette rollers from my local Tesco's because they are cheap. Sadly, my last two Swan rollers have been so badly made it is impossible to roll a decent cigarette, and a third FOC replacement was just as bad!

I enclose all three rollers for your inspection and trial and hope you are willing to send two replacements which work.

The Health Protection Agency
21-12-08

Surveys have shown that people who drink alcohol in modest amounts have better health prospects that those who drink to excess. Surveys have also shown that people who binge on fatty foods and become overweight are more likely to suffer ill health than those who just eat enough for their bodily needs and include fresh fruit and veg in their diet. Statistics also suggest that cigarette smoke is harmful to health and that drugs such as cannabis cause mental illness.

I prefer to view the statistics the other way round. I see the moderate drinker as being at peace with himself and the world and therefore less stressed than the person who drinks to excess. I see the person who binges on fatty foods as having more stress in his life than the person who is content to eat less and feels no need to 'comfort eat'. I see the person who is addicted to cannabis or other hard drugs as someone so stressed he is likely to become mentally ill with or without using drugs for comfort. (In my case I became mentally ill after four terrible months when I was forced to 'sleep rough' on the street and in spite of the fact I was taking no palliative drug at the time.) As for cigarettes, I see a heavy smoker as having less peace of mind, and therefore more stress inside than the person who only smokes once in a while, which would account for the statistics which show that the risk of ill health increases the more heavily one smokes. Meanwhile many life-long smokers live well into old age, their health apparently unaffected, which again suggests it is stress, rather than smoking, which causes ill health.

There are, of course, many causes of stress. including marital breakdown, the loss of a loved one, extreme poverty, business failure, parental abuse in early life, a failed exam, failed love, being bullied in school or the workplace, living alone with no contact from family or friends etc etc - the list is endless. To those who insist that stress has no impact on health I would simply say they can never have known how it feels to be homeless or mentally ill!

So what is the best remedy for stress? I suggest it helps a great deal to be financially secure, but more importantly we need to be deeply valued and loved by a fellow human being, the greatest love being the love known as 'true love' which comes to us all in our teens, but sadly seldom succeeds because it is so under-valued by teachers and parents alike.

To NICE
25-06-07

I still cannot understand why it takes such a long time for some smokers to die from inhaling tobacco smoke, nor why my mother, who had six sons - all of whom smoked, my father too - lived to be ninety-one. Of course, in her day smoking was thought to be harmless.

Sadly, health scares can generate huge amounts of anxiety and fear, as witness the sharp falls in sales of eggs, beef and chicken products, following concerns over salmonella, mad cow disease and chicken flu. When the health scare about smoking began, the relief for those who were able to stop must have been great indeed, while those who continue to smoke must feel anxious and stressed every time they light up a cigarette - unless they've been smoking for many years, with no ill effects at all.

Statistics can be misleading, and in empirical science there simply are no exceptions to laws which have been tested and proved to be true. If it were possible to measure emotional stress, I suspect we would reach very different conclusions on smoking and health from those we are led to believe. With an open mind, we might even begin to search for the causes of stress and acknowledge the impact it has on our health.

by Neville Lewis

**Steven Towndrow
Information Officer
The BMA
9-01-08**

Thank you for your letter of 3rd January, 2008 and enclosures for my information on the risks to health of inhaling tobacco smoke.

I was interested to learn that "doctors can see that their least affluent patients bear the heaviest burden of disease from smoking and second-hand smoke." I have long believed that poverty generates anxiety and sometimes anger, feelings which can lead to poor mental or physical health. Indeed, surveys have shown that rich people are more likely to live beyond the age of 50 than those who are poor, I presume because they are financially more secure and therefore have more peace of mind, while the richer they are, the longer they tend to live. Surveys have also shown that blood pressure levels are higher in unskilled workers than in the more secure managerial or professional classes, which suggests that job insecurity can have an impact on health.

Of course, we all know that emotional stress can arise in a number of ways. Some children are badly affected by strife in the home and or when parents separate, while many become very stressed by our pressurised system of education, where children are told they have "only one chance to succeed", though the morbid effects of 'failure' or fear of 'failure' may not emerge until later in life. I understand that suicides in our society outnumber deaths on our roads and that every day ten people in their twenties take their own lives.

I suggest that our lungs are especially sensitive to stress, which may help explain why asthma is rife in young children these days, in a society where mothers of very young children are encouraged to go out to work and to leave their offspring with carers. A survey has shown that the blood-pressure of breast-fed babies, with their Mums in attendance all day, is one point lower than that of babies fed with a bottle. I guess a survey might well reveal a link between asthma in children and babies left most of the day with child-minders. The shock of bereavement can also affect the health of the lungs, which I presume is the reason why "sharp peaks in mortality rates for infectious and respiratory diseases" occurred during the course of the First World War, presumably as news of the huge numbers of casualties came through from the continent. I suspect this may well be the reason why smoking in females, many of whom had lost loved ones during the Second World War, peaked much later than smoking in males.

Finally, a survey has shown that people who receive hugs from family and friends are less likely to suffer a heart attack than those who never receive such open, impromptu expressions of love.

The Health Protection Agency
3-02-09

Further to my earlier letter regarding the impact of emotional stress on health, which I enclose herewith, I write again on the same subject with particular reference to the perceived impact of smoking and drinking on people's health. When a car or lorry is involved in a collision, we don't blame the vehicle. Instead we normally and rightly blame driver error. By the same token, I believe there is a strong case, as I have stated before, to blame emotional stress for the high incidence of illness in smokers and heavy drinkers, rather than the tobacco smoke or alcohol itself There are many reasons for such an assertion, not least the fact that the incidence of lung cancer in females has failed to fall, despite a significant decline in the number of female smokers from 1974 to 2006, as in males.(Please see graphs enclosed.) Although the incidence of lung cancer in males did fall, I submit that we cannot simply ignore the figures for females if we wish to reach a sound verdict on the impact of smoking on health.

I am convinced we will get a better insight into the main causes of illness if we look deeper into the facts which statistics provide. For example, we know that the role of the female radically changed after the 2nd World War, with most women of working age entering the workplace. Sadly, at the same time there was a loosening of the marital bond as divorce became easier, and many females were left to raise a family on their own, at the same time frequently having to go out to work to make ends meet, while most divorced males had only their own welfare to consider, many of whom were probably hugely relieved to escape from a nagging wife! I believe females have much greater emotional strength than most males, as is shown by the statistics for the incidence of asthma and mental illness in children, which show higher rates for males in all but one instance - please see charts enclosed. (The chart for mental illness also demonstrates the impact of emotional stress on many children's health following family breakdown or the death of a parent.).

Despite their superior emotional strength, I am convinced that most females need the security of a male partner, and that the incidence of lung cancer in females is directly related to the degree of pressure they have been forced to face in recent years. It is also surely significant that more females are drinking in excess of the recommended daily amount, while studies have shown that the gap in life expectancy between females and males has narrowed. Of course some people are more robust than others and therefore are less affected by stress, but I am convinced that the future health of our children depends largely on the formation of happy, lasting relationships, and I enclose an extract from my book, 'The Truth About Love', which gives my final views on the subject and which I hope may engage your interest.

The Medical Research Council
11-08-07

Further to my letter and enclosures of 28-07-07 on the subject of smoking and health, it is surely worth bearing in mind the following facts. Firstly, the majority of smokers - I believe around 90% - never fall ill with lung cancer, in spite of the fact if you blew cigarette smoke into a handkerchief, after a couple of days it would be black as your hat! Secondly, older people, especially pensioners, are much more successful in stopping smoking than those who are young, who have to cope with the huge pressures we place upon them in school and the workplace and also such things as spirally housing costs and the trauma of widespread family breakdown. (Please see statistics enclosed). And thirdly, which is hardly surprising, the Control Theory school of spiritual counselling has discovered a link between suppressed anger and heart disease, which once more supports my belief that emotional stress is the chief cause of ill health in our self-seeking, soulless society today, where we are all taught that all that matters is personal 'success', and where it seems that true happiness is therefore deemed to derive solely from the acquisition of money or social status and fulfilment in one's career.

The Office of Fair Trading
16-01-08

My packet of Drum tobacco states that "smoking seriously harms you and others around you." For many smokers and passive smokers, this statement is simply not true, as many live to a grand old age. I therefore strongly object to such statements, not only because they misrepresent the truth, but also because they engender unnecessary and unfounded anxiety, which is in itself harmful to health, as we know from the results of blood pressure tests.

The health scare on smoking has probably generated more anxiety than any health scare before or since, especially because it is so difficult to stop. I hope you acknowledge that poverty also causes anxiety, which is probably why the incidence of lung cancer is higher than average, and life-expectancy lower, in deprived areas of the UK. If we accept that anxiety can kill, it is surely likely that many who quit smoking are greatly relieved and therefore less likely to fall ill as their fears for their health subside - which is consistent with the statistics - and if they relapse, no doubt their anxiety, and thereby the risk to their health, will return - again as research suggests.

We also know that those who suffer acute anxiety, such as the mentally ill, also tend to be smokers, who find it extremely difficult to stop. If they do manage to quit smoking, some tend to binge on sweet or fatty foods for comfort from stress and often become obese - as is the case with several people I know, who like myself have been mentally ill. In my case, I tend to smoke more than usual when I am angry or anxious, which I suspect is the reason why heavy smokers are more at risk of lung cancer than those who are content to smoke modest amounts. Again this suggests that emotional stress is the real killer, rather than smoking. Why else does the mortality rate for lung cancer in females (many of whom are lone parents on very low incomes) remain stubbornly high, despite a significant fall in numbers of female smokers from 1972 onwards? During that time, it did become easier for males to withdraw from stressful relationships, which may help explain the decline of lung cancer in men, when numbers of male smokers also fell in response to the health scare on smoking.

You may find some of the answers to emotional stress in my book, 'The Truth About Love", which I hammered out on a typewriter in between manic attacks six years ago. In the meantime, it may be wise to recall Churchill's words, "there are lies, damn lies and statistics!"

The Bury Free Press
15-07-07

I have a varied diet and my weight is about right for my height, but I am worried sick that I don't have the recommended five portions of fruit and veg every day. Sometimes I even have fish and chips or fried bacon and egg and I also use salt on some foods, just like my Mum. Sadly, she died in her prime when she was only ninety-one, after indulging herself for many years with full cream milk and sandwiches filled with dripping from the Sunday roast.

Bearing in mind all the foods that are harmful to health, do you think I should stop eating before I become very ill, or just soldier on and hope for the best?

by Neville Lewis

The British Medical Association
18-06-08

Can you please explain why only one in nine smokers die from lung cancer, while millions of smokers live on into old age?

I can only think that the root cause of most serious illness in smokers is stress - which as I have stated before, would help explain why stopping smoking reduces the risk of ill health as anxiety induced by the health scare on smoking imbued in the mind subsides.

With regard to health in general, please find enclosed a brief extract from my book, 'The Truth About Love', which I hope you will read with an open mind.

The Bury Free Press
13-08-07

I am tired of being persecuted for being a smoker for no proven reason at all. Wherever I go, whether to visit my family, a pub or a cafe, I now have to brave the cold, the wind and the rain if I wish to enjoy a smoke.

Since the health scare began, statistics reveal that the mortality rate for lung cancer in females actually rose, from 18.4 per 100,000 population in 1971 to 29.9 per 100,000 in 2002, (the reverse of the trend for males), despite a dramatic decline in numbers of female smokers over the same period, just as for males.

I see no sense in any empirical search for the truth which is entirely based on the facts which seem to support the hypothesis, while blithely ignoring the rest, so I guess I will just have to remain a social pariah out in the cold until our scientists and researchers acknowledge the impact on health of emotional stress, which hits women much harder than men when relationships fail, as they did in huge numbers around the same time as the health scare on smoking began.

Meanwhile, of course, around nine out of ten smokers never fall ill with lung cancer, and many (as well as passive smokers) live to a grand old age.

The British Medical Association
7-3-08

My pack of tobacco tells me that smoking causes ageing of the skin How true that is - as I have noticed in many people who continue to smoke into their 70's or 80's, despite government warnings. Many such people no doubt would live well into their hundreds, if they saw sense and stopped smoking.

Yesterday I met a sad young man at my local pub as we sat outside in the cold having a drink and a smoke. He said he had taken the day off to relax, as his job was extremely stressful. He said he ran his own business and worked twelve hours every day, so it made sense to relax now and then. He made the excuse that his grandfather smoked and lived well into his nineties. (How sad, I thought - he could have lived to a hundred and fifty!) The young man even maintained that the laws about smoking were stupid!
For my part, I explained that I was retired and lived alone without love or companionship, so I wasn't too worried how long I had left to live.,,

The British Medical Association
21-02-08

I understand that I may soon need a licence to smoke, at the discretion of my GP.

Why should I be persecuted for smoking - which is a comfort to me as a mentally sick person aged 68 on a small pension - when we all know that many smokers live to a grand old age?

Much illness is associated with smoking, but the same can be said for stress, and I have been mentally ill most of my life. I have nonetheless worked and paid taxes the whole of my life, apart from a few years when I was very ill after having been homeless.

I live on my own and I make no demands of anyone else in the community. I have few pleasures, as my medication affects my quality of life, but I do enjoy my 'roll-ups'. If I am not even allowed to smoke in my declining years, neither outside nor in my flat, I might as well throw in the towel!

by Neville Lewis

The British Medical Association
19-05-08

If the capacity to cope with emotional stress has nothing to do with ill health, why is it that females tend to live longer than males, while millions of life-long smokers live well into old age?

I suggest that those who receive plenty of love when they are young are also less likely to suffer ill health in later years, whether or not they happen to smoke. Of course a great deal of stress is also caused by financial hardship, as well as the pressures induced by our system of education and the moronic obsession with wealth and possessions which grips our greedy, self-seeking society today.

As I firmly believe and have stated before, only the miracle of love, and with it the sharing of wealth, can bring the prospect of greatly improved mental and physical health for our children in years to come.

Copies
NICE
The Health Protection Agency
Cancer Research UK
The British Heart Foundation

The Health Protection Agency
23-03-08

I once learned of an orphanage for babies in Eastern Europe where every child was listless, with few responses - except for the one nearest the door, who always received a spontaneous hug from the nurse as she left.

A survey in the UK has also shown that those who receive hugs are less likely to suffer a heart attack later in life - such is the power of love.

My own heart attack came in my fifties.

The Bury Free Press
12-3-07

A recent survey claims that some business managers behave like psychopaths in the way they bully their staff. Meanwhile, if an employee cannot cope with such abuse, and is so upset that he quits his job with no other job to go to, he has to wait six weeks before he can claim the dole .It is therefore hardly surprising that many people who eke out a living on benefit prefer to remain as they are, rather than face the pressures and insecurity of today's workplace and a possible 'black hole' in their finances. They know full well that they may forced to steal just to survive, or in the case of those who have mental health problems, relapse and fall ill with the stress, which in turn may lead to a jail sentence or hospitalisation, at great expense to the state.

The dole system, of course, is based on the paranoid premise that people are naturally lazy, which is simply not the case. In the sixties it was easy to go from job to job, whatever the state of your health, because there was full employment, and employers were desperate for staff. Today there is fierce competition for work in many regions of the UK, so the long-term sick or unemployed are seriously disadvantaged in the hunt for a job. I just hope our Government's plan to force the long-term unemployed and some of our mentally sick back into work doesn't misfire. It is easy to kick a man when he's down, but it's not so easy to pick up the pieces when such a policy fails, as well it may if decisions involving a person's fitness for work are left in the hands of ruthless, private entrepreneurs!

I suggest that without full employment the cynical scheme, as a cost-cutting exercise, will in any case prove to be totally counter-productive.

Chris Grayling MP
Minister of State for Work and Pensions
12-6-11

I hope you agree that some people have much more drive and confidence than others and therefore are more able to get into and stay in work than the many who languish on state benefit, through no fault of their own, because of the fierce competition for jobs in an employers' market. In 1961, when there was virtually full employment, the economy was booming, few people needed to claim benefit to live and employers were desperate for staff and to retain them, it was extremely easy to find work. In my case, although I was heavily sedated after a severe mental breakdown, I was able to get into work with no difficulty at all, which I know is the fervent wish of the vast majority who currently eke out a living on benefit.

I wish you would get it into your head and that of all your compatriots in government, that no child is born inherently lazy, whatever his situation may be and however badly a tiny minority abuses the benefits system. I suggest if you used all your muscle and might to get the economy booming again, you would be making far better use of the talents with which you were born. It is the only sane and sensible way to reduce the huge burden of welfare payments which currently exists and which is entirely due to the state of the economy - and for no other reason under the sun! Your jaundiced view of the human psyche can only lead to terrible pain and injustice for many who may be judged to be fit for work, when they are simply not able to cope with the pressures applied by many employers in the current state of the labour market. I earnestly hope common sense will prevail and that you and all those in government with a paranoid outlook will think again!

Chris Grayling MP
Minister of State for Work and Pensions
14-6-11

The widespread breakdown of relationships in our society in recent years, resulting in a third of the population living alone, has led to an acute shortage of housing, which has triggered a huge escalation in the cost of a home, while wage levels have lagged far behind with the virtual death of the unions in an employers' market, with so many citizens unemployed. At the same time there has been a huge increase in the number of females obliged to work, to help with the cost of housing, as well as a necessary increase in housing support for the many whose wages have failed to keep pace with the rise in house prices.

We may not be able to do much to improve relationships, but a female acquaintance recently told me that she and most of her female friends would much rather remain in the home to take of their young and their ageing relatives, which they see as their natural, caring role and which would hugely improve their quality of life and that of their families. Sadly, she said that the cost of housing forced them to work. I submit if we had a booming economy, employers would be obliged to attract and retain staff by increasing the wages they offer, to the point where a home became much more affordable on one person's wage, as in times past, allowing the female in any partnership to pursue her preferred role in the home. At the same time, with less income from females available for rent or mortgages, the relative cost of a home would continue to fall to an acceptable level. Meanwhile, of course, the huge burden of welfare payments the taxpayer currently bears would substantially reduce, as I said in my earlier letter, without cutting costs across the board, as is proposed now, causing great hardship and suffering to thousands of vulnerable fellow-citizens, while others continue to live in a state of relative luxury.

I see no reason why we should not have a booming economy in the near future, given the needs of a rapidly developing world and the great advantage our nation has with its knowledge and expertise. Having said that, we should, of course, never exceed our income again or allow greedy bankers to indulge in speculative ventures which can create havoc with the economy whenever they fail!

The Rt Hon David Ruffley MP
9-01-08

I was extremely concerned to hear of the Conservatives' plan to force people on incapacity benefit, and the long-term unemployed, to train for work or engage in community work, on pain of losing their benefit. If benefit is stopped, for whatever reason, how on earth can the person or persons concerned be expected to survive?

I am convinced that the majority of people on benefit would love to get back into work, to improve their income and thereby their quality of life, but they know only too well, often from hard experience, that the chance of being offered a job is remote, simply because there are invariably other candidates with a better track record in terms of health and work history. In my case, after having been homeless and then very ill for a time, I was turned down for shelf-filling work, pushing trolleys and even distributing leaflets, so there was no chance of getting back to the work I was used to, which was computerised accounts, although I did try.

The only work I could get was delivering newspapers, for something like three pounds an hour. Sadly, three fifths of my weekly earnings went back to the local Council by way of reduced Housing and Council Tax benefit, while the 16-hour rule meant that I couldn't take on any more rounds without losing my incapacity benefit, so I was stuck like a rat in a poverty-trap. In any case, I became so vexed, confused and frustrated with all the bureaucracy, just over a couple of paper-rounds, that I soon ended up back in hospital - and that was the last work I ever did.

The Guardian
28-07-08

Surveys have shown that 90% of people who eke out a living on incapacity benefit would love to get back into work if the jobs were there, so I see no need for a 'stick' to be wielded as well as a 'carrot' to help meet their need. In private hands I am sure that a 'stick' would become a cudgel, which would inadvertently put many stable but vulnerable mentally sick people back into hospital for weeks or months at a time, at considerable cost to the NHS, not to mention the suffering of all those affected.

by Neville Lewis

In 1961 there were just 275,000 on the dole, compared with 1.6 million today Jobs were secure and work was widely available. If the same labour market prevailed today I am certain that the majority we currently see 'trapped' on incapacity benefit would be in regular work and paying their way in society. As things are, employers are bound to recruit staff from the dole queue in preference to those with a history of illness.

We already have severe penalties for those who make fraudulent benefit claims As likely as not some will still seek to milk 'the system' until they get caught, just as some of our silver-tongued, honourable members of Parliament have been found misusing expense accounts.or raising funds through the wrong channels.

Copies:
Marjorie Wallace
The Mental Health Foundation
MIND
Alan Johnson MP Sec of State for Health
The BMA
Clare Short MP
Baroness Williams
David Ruffley MP
John Humphrys
Polly Toynbee
James Purnell MP Sec of State for Work and Pensions

'Feedback'
BBC Radio 4
11-11-08

I listened with interest to the Radio 4 programme entitled 'Incapacitated' and I sympathise deeply with anyone who has lost his job and possibly also his home as a result of the current financial crisis. It is a traumatic experience to have one's income reduced to the level of the dole, so it is hardly surprising that some victims become so depressed that their doctors prescribe tablets and issue sick notes to help with the stress of their situation. In my case, when I suffered an acute attack of anxiety and depression at the age of 21, my mother urged me to try to find work and I was lucky, because at that time, in 1961, there was virtually full employment, with just 275, 000 receiving the dole As a result, some employers were desperate for staff and would take on anyone who was willing to work, whatever the state of their health, and often a job was a job for life. I therefore quickly found work and remained in continuous employment until I was 58, when I fell ill again and was hospitalised several times.

As I began to recover, I tried my utmost to get back into work, but I was turned down for shelf-filling work, pushing trolleys and even for a job delivering leaflets, and the only work I could get was a newspaper round. I did try for a job in computerised accounts, which was my speciality, but I failed to get a reply, presumably because of my history of illness and because at the time there were more than a million on the dole with a clean bill of health competing for work. In the end, I became so demoralised that I fell ill again and from then on until my retirement date I did no more work and remained trapped on incapacity benefit.

I entirely agree with the programme that being in work is good for one's health, but until and unless we have full employment, as in 1961, I am sure there will remain many who languish on incapacity benefit for years to come, the same as the long-term unemployed who subsist on the dole. In my case, I am happier now I'm retired and secure with my State Pension, and I can look the world in the eye with my self-esteem restored, but only thanks to the passage of time!
Sadly, full employment, which we all wish for, empowers the unions, while high unemployment gives power to the Government and leaders of industry, in the age-long struggle for the maximum share of the national cake. Meanwhile those with the weakest voice frequently go to the wall.

Edward Young
Office of the Leader of the Opposition
5-01-08

Thank you for your letter of 31st January, in reply to mine of January 9th.

To tell the truth, I am amazed and disgusted to hear our well-heeled, privileged, silver-tongued politicians complaining about a perceived 'something for nothing' culture, which they imagine exists in the least-privileged, most vulnerable members of our society - i.e. the sick and the long-term unemployed.

As one of my sons jokingly says, "you've got to kick a man when he's down!"
and the proposed draconian threat to deny such unfortunates the means to live and even their right to a home - as also proposed by Labour - almost beggars belief!

I submit that we all have a God-given value as human beings, with an inalienable right to be loved and looked after right from the start by the society in which we live - especially when we fall ill or become unemployed.

by Neville Lewis

Mrs H Payne
Department for Work and Pensions
28-03-08

Thank you for your letter of 26 March 2008 in reply to my letter to the Secretary of State, Mr Purnell.

Although I myself am retired, I hope that no penalties will be applied to any person currently receiving incapacity benefit, who after reflection fails to take up the proposed work-related activities scheme. I know several severely-sick, heavily sedated mental health patients who would almost certainly relapse and end up once more in hospital (at great cost to the NHS) if they came under pressure, in spite of the fact they may appear perfectly normal and sane when assessed.

Can you please confirm that no pressure by way of penalties - or the threat of penalties - will be applied in such cases?

Copies:
Alan Johnson MP, Secretary of State for Health
Marjorie Wallace c/o SANE
The Mental Health Foundation
David Cameron MP, Leader of the Opposition

Mike Whitworth
Department for Work and Pensions
9-05-08

Thank you for your letter of 7th May, 2008, in which you state that "people with fluctuating medical conditions will not be penalised if they feel unable to take part in the work-related activities which we are now proposing."

By inference, there will clearly be penalties for some at the discretion of the department, in spite of the fact that you freely admit that "there may be instances where the fluctuating nature of a person's medical condition is not known to the ESA decision maker!" You then say that "in such instances any evidence presented on the claimant's behalf indicating a change in the severity of their condition will be looked at sympathetically by the decision maker."

How naive can you get? For most mentally sick patients "a change in the severity of their condition" only becomes obvious when they are admitted to hospital under section, often for weeks or months at a time, and I am convinced from my own experience of mental illness that any savings in benefit payments will be hugely out-stripped by the extra cost to the NHS and Social Services as they are compelled to deal with the victims of the new scheme.

It would be nice if people like you, along with our politicians, lived in the real world, or at least had a heart, but no doubt the huge likely cost to the NHS will go unnoticed by the Department for Work and Pensions, who will claim widespread success in reducing their costs!

The Rt Hon James Purnell MP
Sec of State for Work and Pensions
12-12-08

Dear Mr Purnell,

I understand that nearly every sick person of working age who is living on benefit will soon face pressure from a 'personal advisor' to get back into work I must say I am thankful I am retired, because I know what it is like to be heavily sedated after being in hospital under section a number of times. Most mentally sick patients are treated with powerful tranquillisers, which not only impair concentration but also induce feelings of tiredness and lethargy, making any prolonged activity a struggle and an ordeal. Too much pressure can easily lead to another 'trip' back to hospital - in my case after taking on just a couple of paper rounds - the only work I could get after having been ill.

I accept that 90% of people living on benefit would love to get back into work, but I suggest that many of our mentally sick patients who are forced to exchange the security of the benefits system for the pressures and insecurity of the world of work will likely sink, rather than swim. I suspect many will be swept back into hospital, at great cost to the NHS and Social Services, unless, of course, they are so desperate they take the final way out!

I presume 'personal advisors' will be paid according to results??

by Neville Lewis

The Rt Hon David Cameron MP
Leader of the Opposition
6-05-08

After 25 years of marital misery, I separated from my wife and we are much happier now, as merely good friends. There simply are no financial inducements which could persuade me to live with the lady again, and I am surprised that the Conservatives seem to believe that marriage promotes longer-lasting relationships.

Please be assured that affairs of the heart, when we fall in love with that special person for us, have nothing to do with money or status and that couples truly 'in love' would never live apart, however much they might stand to gain from the benefits system.

We all fall in love in our teens with that special person for us, but the pressures of education stand in the way of any real chance of success, so most of us have to make do with a less than perfect and often stressful relationship in later life - which is a sad reflection indeed on our system of education and on our core values as a society.

29-08-10

On the Importance of Love over Money

The sign of a woman in love shows in her eyes, which shine like stars whenever she looks at her man, while he in his turn knows an exquisite, deep inner peace and the feeling that he could conquer Everest with ease!

To help mend our 'broken' society, our Government naively has promised financial inducements to keep couples together, however strained their relationships may be - as if money can buy me love. Sadly, I see many long faces but few starry-eyed couples in my home town - a town typically obsessed with what money may do.

I cannot understand why the act of sex should be regarded by teachers and law-makers as some kind of sweet or lollipop they expect to be widely indulged in after a period of enforced abstinence, rather than the natural consummation of love which follows a period of courtship and naturally leads to one sexual partner for life. If we would like to see real social change, teachers should surely tell children, especially the girls, what it feels like to be 'in love' - rather than merely 'attracted' - and how they should go about seeing their love succeed. After all, times have changed. It's not 'a man's world' any more and in any case females have much more courage than males in matters of love! Most people can be perfectly happy on little money, providing they have the right partner in life or are surrounded with love by family and friends - and 'true love' significantly comes to us all in our teens...

If such love in our young was widely successful, I submit it would hugely benefit their physical and mental health and that of their fortunate children in years to come by averting the damaging stress which so often arises from broken or troubled relationships - not to mention the health risks involved in a culture of casual, promiscuous sex, which currently accounts for 200,000 abortions and a half-million cases of sexually-transmitted disease (mainly in females), in the UK every year - at huge cost to the NHS.

I guess it is small wonder that some self-respecting young men prefer to remain celibate!

Gordon Brown MP
Prime Minister
22-08-07

If relationships in our society were based on the love which comes to us all around the time of puberty, I suggest they would remain firm and true. There would be no need for three million more homes to be built, as many females, with so much love in their hearts, would opt to remain in the home to take care of their young and their ageing parents.

When we receive love, we give out love, and well-loved children grow into caring, responsible adults, so there would be less crime or anti-social behaviour in years to come, with huge potential savings in policing, judicial and penal costs.

Most people are happy inside when they receive love from both parents right from the start, and happy people are less likely to be mentally ill or addicted to drink or drugs or to binge on food for comfort from stress. Hence there would be huge savings in health care costs in future years if relationships were based on real love, rather than superficial attraction.

So why don't we support and encourage 'true love' in our young when it comes - the most valuable, beautiful gift we can ever receive in our lives? If homework, which is so stressful for some, was optional, our children would have much more time to mingle and meet with the opposite sex and to see their love blossom and grow. After all, most of the knowledge we gain in the scramble for qualifications, unless it retains our interest, is soon lost to memory through lack of use, so most of our effort, and that of our teachers, is frequently wasted! In any case, what use is knowledge or intellect without any love, if all it leads to is unbridled greed for money, status or power and the cruel, self-seeking society we live in today?

Sadly, as an American president once said, we cannot legislate for the way people feel, however much we attempt to control their lives.

The Rt Hon David Ruffley MP
12-07-08

Thank you for your letter in response to mine to The Times.

As you must know, surveys suggest that our children are the most unhappy children in Europe, despite our society's great wealth. Nonetheless, with the right approach to their emotional needs, I submit that they could be the happiest in the world - happiness mainly consisting in loving and being loved by one's partner, family and friends, while having, of course, enough guaranteed income to cover one's needs.

We all fall in love around the time of puberty and we can all recall the name of the loved one the rest of our lives, but first love seldom succeeds, partly because its superlative value is widely denied and partly because of the pressures involved in our system of education, which often asks more than our children can give and even makes some of them seriously ill, poor devils.

If our children are to be happy, I suggest they should have the same choices as adults, and therefore that homework, as I have stated before, should be optional by statute for every child in the land. At least that way our children will have the chance to meet with the opposite sex every day after school and hopefully see their love blossom and flower when they find themselves falling in love. (Just for the record, you might tell Jim Knight that happy children make the best learners and that 'true love' is the most inspiring, enabling feeling we know, so standards would probably rise!)

Our children are our future, but if all that they learn in school about life is to be self-seeking individuals, with scant thought or concern for the needs of others, they may never learn what it is to be truly happy, however much wealth they obtain for themselves and whatever heights they aspire to in terms of social status in years to come.

It is said it is better to give than to receive, as Bill Gates has begun to discover, so what else should we seek, if not to be truly happy?

Anatomy of a Society

Copies:
Polly Toynbee
Marjorie Wallace
Clare Short MP

The British Medical Association
16-04-08

True love is the most beautiful, inspiring, enduring love known to man and is presented to everyone during their teens, yet its value is widely denied by parents and teachers alike, who place much greater emphasis on education. As a result, early love frequently fails and often leads to an orgy of sexual encounters, with scant thought for the health risks involved or the feelings of those who get hurt, nor for the longer-term damage to mental and physical health.

I am certain a survey of elderly couples who became childhood sweethearts, with one sexual partner in life, would clearly show that relationships based on true love, and formed when we are young, offer the best possible chance for a happy life free from ill health.

The Rt Hon David Ruffley MP
6-09-07

Thank you for your letter of 4-09-07, in which you ask if there are any specific issues I would like you to take up.

First, I would like you to campaign for homework to be made optional by statute for all our children in schools and for odious 'league tables' to be scrapped, for reasons explained in my booklet, 'The Truth About Love'. Second, I would like to see the contraceptive pill made available free of charge at all chemists and major stores for all girls under the age of sixteen, so as to reduce the number of abortions which currently take place in our society - 186,000 last year alone - and also because a third of 'mature' children under sixteen quite naturally experience the act of sex. Second, I would like you to press for a change in the law which would enable mentally sick people who have enough courage to seek work, to do so without any risk to their existing level of disposable income, even if they are given the sack by a future employer or simply cannot cope and end up on the penury of the dole - in which case they should have their former benefits restored with immediate effect, with no stressful forms to fill in again Third, in St Edmundsbury I would like you to press for the availability of 'affordable' homes to be restricted

by Neville Lewis

to first-time buyers on a points basis according to need, with priority given to those who live and work in the borough, in the same fashion as is applied to those who are homeless, thereby avoiding an escalation in price of 'affordable' homes due to market pressures as more people move into the region.. At the same time, at national level, I would like to see the purchase of homes to let made illegal, as well as the purchase of holiday homes in areas where there is known to be a shortage of affordable homes for the local population.

Last but not least, I would like you to press for a return to the benefits system where state support is provided when it is needed and not in arrears, especially for those who become homeless, not just in terms of money for food, but also for temporary accommodation to be always available from a pool of landlords and landladies paid direct by the local council concerned, so that no-one need suffer a single night 'sleeping rough' out in the open because all the hostels and homes for the homeless are full. A man who used to work with the homeless once told me that for every month that a person is forced to 'sleep rough' on the street, it takes him a year to recover. In my case I never did until many years had passed.

If you press for the changes outlined above, I suspect you will likely become infamous and lose your seat in the Commons at the next general election. On the other hand, you might just become famous for spear-heading a much-needed change in the principles by which we live!

David Beal
Office of the Leader of the Opposition
30-08-08

Thank you for your letter of 26-08-08, in which you quote Nick Gibb as saying, "It simply isn't good enough that the educational divide between rich and poor is so wide." (More importantly, it is also worth noting that life expectancy is known to be substantially lower in deprived parts of the UK, sometimes by as much as two decades compared to that of more affluent citizens!)

With respect to educational differences, I submit that passing the buck on to the schools themselves, as Conservatives plan to do, by "making schools accountable to parents in order to improve opportunities for all children", totally fails to address the problem, which is the stress of poverty itself. A 'Robin Hood' approach by Government, to take from the rich and give to the poor, is clearly the only remedy, but who in our self-seeking, loveless society is willing to part with a penny to help the poor, including our 'honourable' politicians?

Anatomy of a Society

To a dear AA Friend
5-07-10

The first intimation I had that 'something was up' in the way of contact with God through music came when I happened to borrow a CD by Paul Robeson, a singer my father used to admire, from the local library. It began with the words, "Look up, look up and seek your Maker, for Gabriel blows his horn. True love, true love, what have I done that you should grieve me so? You caused me to walk and talk like I never done before!" Had I not desperately sought to hand my will and my life over to God many months before? Had I not recently walked hundreds of miles on country footpaths to try to get over my love for Shirley? (I have disguised her real name) And had I not written reams on my Step 4 of the programme of Alcoholics Anonymous and to various people on the subject of love? Paul Robeson also goes on to sing about "big, high mountains" - I had just returned from a holiday in Scotland, where somehow I had managed to climb Ben Nevis and Ben Lomond after having had a heart attack in my fifties and being sat at a desk for most of my working life! There were also other sections of the album with which I could closely relate.

The crucial turning point in my life had come not long before when I had managed to forgive my poor father, whom I had hated and even wanted to kill with a knife when I was a very young boy because of the way he treated my mother, on whom I depended for love. Sadly, it was only much later in life, when I did my Step 4 of the programme and had counselling which took me right back to early childhood, that I discovered my father wasn't completely to blame and that both my mother and father were badly affected by the war, and that prior to that they had been completely happy together.. Forgiving my father came as a huge relief and feelings of anger, which had festered inside for years, were finally released and replaced by feelings of love.

My mother, of course, had often retaliated in anger at the way she was treated by my father -although there was no violence on either side -and I felt so angry with both my parents at times that when I went to church to be confirmed I felt I didn't deserve the blessing of the Holy Spirit. (I couldn't help thinking about what I had read in the bible - "Honour thy father and thy mother that thy days may be long in the land thy Lord giveth thee." I didn't honour them then, but I do now, because their intentions were good and I hope we all meet in Heaven someday.

On the Bob Dylan disk, there is a passage which says, "Ships sailing in through the mist, you were born with a snake in both of your fists, while a hurricane was blowing.- freedom just around the corner for you." (I was born in August 1939, just a month before we entered the war which was raging in Europe)

by Neville Lewis

The Bury Free Press
21-09-08

For all walkers and cyclists and those who would like to lose a few pounds, I can wholeheartedly recommend the cycle path between Bury and Thurston, which some of your readers may not know exists.

Proceeding along Eastgate Street and then walking the challenging hill up Mount Road, you are greeted with wonderful views of the town. Then follows a shaded, leafy section which eventually leads to open country as you pass the last houses of the sprawling Moreton Hall estate. Passing the Flying Fortress pub, where you may wish to rest for a while and take some refreshment, the path then skirts the Rougham Airfield, where sometimes model aeroplanes may be seen doing daring manoeuvres on a fine day, or indeed real aeroplanes taking off and landing.. When the path ends, a quiet little lane takes you on to a crossing over the railway and before you know it houses appear on one side of the road and you know you have made it to Thurston. If you wish you can celebrate your achievement with a pint at the Fox and Hounds pub and then catch the bus back to Bury. There is even a station a few steps away for those who prefer travelling by train.

It's a splendid walk, which I have done several times, but sadly few people seem to make use of the path unless, like me, they are keen walkers or cyclists or cannot afford a car.

The Bury Free Press
15-12-09

I hate being a kill-joy, but where is the sense in relatives and friends feeling obliged to exchange cards and presents of more or less equal value to those they expect in return every Christmas, whether or not there is contact between them the rest of the year?

I have always believed it is 'the thought' that counts and not the amount of money we feel we should spend in a monotonous ritual which can be considerably stressful, not knowing for sure how our gifts will be received!

There is no way that love can be expressed in terms of money, unless there is no expectation of a return, as was the case of the Good Samaritan - whether or not the story is true. And so may I wish you, your staff and your readers a Christmas and a New Year filled with love.

Anatomy of a Society

Dear Shirley,
12-12-11

Although I dread your response to this letter, I must be allowed to explain why I thought your life and mine had in some way been preordained and predicted in song, before we were even born. As you know, I first became aware of peculiar coincidences on hearing songs by Paul Robeson and then more emphatically songs by Bob Dylan, which I implored you to hear when I moved into the caravan in Beyton. Naturally, you must have thought I was losing my marbles, bearing in mind I had stopped the drugs I had been taking for such a large part of my life - although I had been free from such drugs for nearly two years. Please bear with me while I list some of the main coincidences which struck me so forcibly, after which I hope at least you may acquit me of being insane at the time - in spite of the fact I later fell ill due to the terrible stress I came under when I ran out of money and was homeless for such a long time, when all I could think of for most of each day was where to go next in search of support and where I could safely spend the night.

My brief list is as follows and I leave you to make up your own mind as to the meaning and implications of so many unusual coincidences, which in this instance appeared in Bob Dylan's album entitled 'Infidels', a copy of which I sent you earlier this year. For example:

"You were born with a snake in both of your fists while a hurricane was blowing" - I was born just a month before Britain entered the war which was raging in Europe and I remember my mother and father were constantly arguing fiercely when I was a small child.

"Sugarman bays to the nightingale tune; goodbye hi by the light of the moon." - As you know, 'sugar' is sometimes used as a word for 'drug', while the 'nightingale tune' seemed to refer to the letters of love which I gave you so often before saying goodbye and heading for Scotland, sleeping for much of the time in the open in my sleeping bag, i.e. "by the light of the moon". Similarly, the following passage appears later: "Resting in the fields, far from the turbulent space; have a sleep 'neath the stars with a smile dumb lit in your face." - I did smile to myself at times while writing the caustic comments I made in some of my letters deploring my situation when I was homeless!

"Fools rush in, where angels fear to tread, both of the future so full of dread - you don't show one, shedding off one more layer of skin, keeping one step ahead of the prosecutor within." - I think I can be forgiven for thinking this referred to the

by Neville Lewis

moment I felt a bit wobbly in the office and briefly piped my eye before going on holiday to Scotland, bearing in mind I feared that I might not make it back because of the state of my heart. The 'prosecutor within' seemed to refer to my wretched conscience regarding my love for you.

"Friend to the martyr, friend to the woman of shame" - Sorry, but I couldn't help thinking of Eric in the office and yourself - Eric always blaming himself for everything that went wrong in his life.

"You rise up and say goodbye to no-one" - This seemed to refer to the moment I felt very faint while walking during my holiday in Scotland, when I hastened by taxi to the Glasgow Infirmary, where I said I thought I was about to suffer a heart attack. They gave me an ECG and the nurse afterwards said 'there was nothing wrong with me' and 'why was I wasting their time?' I was amazed, but hugely relieved, of course.

Later the same night, I happened to wander quite unawares into the red light district of Glasgow, where I was solicited for sex, first by young men in cars and then by several young girls on a building site. You may imagine my surprise on my return from Scotland when later I heard the following passage from the same album: "You're going to Sodom and Gomorrah, but what do you care, aint nobody there would want to marry your sister!"

- I had no sisters.

"You're a man of the mountains, a man of the clouds etc" - This, of course, after I happened to have climbed Ben Lomand and Ben Nevis while on holiday, seemed again to anticipate more of my actions, which astonished me at the time.

All these strange coincidences appeared on the first track of the album and many more on other tracks, but I won't try your patience with any more examples. Heaven knows how I came to acquire it. I just can't remember.

However, I must mention that the second track and some which followed seemed in my mind to refer to you. "A smile so hard to resist" and "What's a sweetheart like you doing in a dump like this?" and "You know news of you has come down the line even before you came in the door" and the passage, "Got to be an important person to be in here honey; got to have done some evil deed; got to have your own hell when you come in the door; got to play your harp till your lips bleed!" all seemed to suggest that you, like myself, had no control over any events in your life, as if they had all been preordained. Other parts of the track did seem to prophesy a much happier future for you, even riches and fame!

But of course, I suppose in truth all the coincidences I have recalled, and many more by other singers, which I won't mention here, could refer to anyone, whether real or fictional. I merely hope, as I stated before, that at least I may be acquitted of being insane at the time. I guess I'm a fool to write this letter, but I just wanted to try if I could to set the record straight.

Hoping you have a very happy Christmas.

Sincerely yours etc.

The Rt Hon Clare Short MP
12-12-07

During one of my 'manic' attacks after having been homeless, I really believed I was striding straight into hell, to face everlasting, unbearable pain in every sinew and nerve of my body. Yet throughout my terrifying ordeal, I was somehow sustained by a glimmer of hope that somehow, someday I might get to see the woman I loved - at a happier time and place!

I simply cannot believe there is any such place as a hell after death. It just wouldn't make any sense, because none of us has any choice in being born, nor any control over the people or the events which shape and mould our thoughts and feelings in early life, which I am convinced have a huge influence on the way that we act and behave in later years.

At least we do know that there is such a thing as 'true love' and that love is the greatest healer of all. It is also my firm belief that we are all born with love in our hearts and that we all need and deserve to be loved from the start, because we all have a value as human beings. Even Hitler was surely once an innocent little boy - until he was beaten nearly to death by his Dad, and taunted by his peers. When we receive love, we respond with love, and it seems to me only love can change our world into a better place fit for our children in years to come.

In my case there is only one woman I truly love, but since I've been ill she has failed to respond to my letters, in which I have expressed how I feel many times. I once heard a song by Matt Munro called 'The Unreachable Star', which you may know. It includes the words, "to love, pure and chaste, from afar", and also the words, "to be willing to march into hell for a heavenly cause." I hope I can be forgiven for once thinking the words were 'intended' for me! Thankfully, I no longer harbour such thoughts in my head and I've had no more painful 'escapes from reality' for nearly four years. But I do have a penchant for writing, which I guess you know only too well!

The Economist
21-1-12

What does it really matter if a few banks should fail due to their reckless lending for profit, which has led to massive national debts and severe hardship for many as austerity measures are applied in an attempt to rectify the situation? Trade and industry worldwide will continue as ever, albeit tragically at a much slower pace than before. Have we not seen down-turns in economic activity before for the same basic reason - i.e. because banks are managed for profit, when they should be run as a free service to the community, funded by the state on a sane and sensible basis by universal consent? How else can we expect to obtain the financial stability necessary for sustained growth in the global economy?

After all, money in essence is merely a means of exchanging useful goods and services, not a tool which by itself can create wealth. Clearly banks in their current form, trading in money for profit and competing with everyone's money in markets governed by fickle confidence, do more harm than good. The world's capacity for growth can only be driven by its industrial output, not by banks gambling on a grand scale with its means of exchange, which so often leads to damaging cycles of 'boom and bust', leading to drastic reductions in vital investment and credit to business worldwide.

Only the world's leaders acting in unison with courage and determination can provide a financial system which truly serves the needs of the community, instead of itself, and so bring the stability we so badly need. As long as overpaid, invulnerable bankers, with their myopic vision obscured by unbridled greed for profit, remain unaccountable to the wider public, so long will millions of innocent, vulnerable citizens continue to suffer the consequences of such a flawed financial system!

Why is it so few seem to acknowledge this simple truth?

Copies: The London School of Economics; The Governor, The Bank of England
Polly Toynbee; Boris Johnson; Ed Miliband MP

Evan Davis; The Centre for Policy Studies
Hugh Pym; The Institute of Economic Affairs
The Commons Treasury Select Committee
The Chairman, The CBI

26-1-12
To all concerned,

Please may I add my further thoughts regarding the current financial system, following my letter of 21-1-12, which I attach for your reference.

By "a free service to the community", I don't necessarily rule out some measure of interest on loans to fund wages and salaries etc, but that banks' operations should no longer be run for profit, with strict limits on how much capital can be employed to provide mortgages etc and loans and long-term investments to business to boost the economy. Any surplus revenue could then go to the Exchequer, rather than into the pockets of shareholders or greedy, self-serving staff by way of massive bonuses. We have already seen how gambling for a quick profit in company capital led to the dreadful Wall Street Crash and the Great Depression of the 30's, as well as the recent credit squeeze which resulted from the debacle caused by excessive lending by banks for profit in the sub-prime mortgage market At the same time, as fickle confidence plummeted, the value of company capital on the stock exchanges in the US and the UK fell by as much as a third overnight, a value which bore no relation to the real, book value of listed companies, but nonetheless caused major problems for them and their suppliers, as we all know.

I see no reason why banks should not be run as a reliable, dependable service to the community with no profit motive involved, their operatives accountable to the state and hence the taxpayer, with strict rules to prevent high risk initiatives, which can so easily lead to disaster for the wider economy, as millions of jobs are lost and all that such a scenario means to the quality of life of all who are affected.

I appreciate such a radical change to the system would require worldwide consensus, but I am convinced the benefits to trade and industry and everyone's quality of life would be substantial and ongoing.

by Neville Lewis

OFSTED
23-01-12

While a pupil at Sudbury Grammar School in Suffolk, I received constant glowing reports on my progress and was told I should easily obtain a first class degree in Oxford or Cambridge University. In the end, after two years at university in London, I suffered a serious breakdown, mainly due to fear of failing, and was unable to continue the course. As a result, I saw myself as 'a failure' in my career and for many years sought consolation in alcohol. As we know, there are some who, when they fail to obtain a particular 'qualification', such as a longed-for 'grade' or 'degree', prefer to commit suicide. Bearing in mind there is no absolute level of attainment where learning is concerned and that prestigious degrees or grades are only awarded on a comparative, arbitrary basis, I see no reason why anyone should be deemed to have failed in the learning process, nor why so much should be made to depend on the outcome of a few stressful exams after years of painstaking study. To give all our young some sense of achievement, however little or much they may learn at the time, given their own limitations and varied abilities, I suggest the following, or similar awards would be far more appropriate to the need - for example:

"This is to certify that Joe Bloggs has obtained considerable knowledge in History, his chosen subject at university, for which he deserves every congratulation." OR... "This is to certify that Joe Bloggs has obtained considerable knowledge of History (and or any other subject or skill) while still at school etc" OR even, "This is to certify that Joe Bloggs, to his credit and with much effort, has succeeded in mastering the basic 3R's of reading, writing and arithmetic."

by John Powell

"Psychologists, in studying human motivation, have found that positive reinforcements of the will, (reward for good conduct) are infinitely more effective than negative reinforcements (punishment for bad conduct). To be constantly critical of a person is obviously a dangerous thing. It tends to undermine his confidence and make all authority obnoxious. However, if one takes the approach of positive reinforcements, tending to overlook small failures in conduct but never failing to recognise and reward (at least with a kind word) the desired conduct, the effect will be almost magical. It is an illustration of the power released in the creation of good self-image. Most people will be in their conduct what we tell them they are."

The same, of course, applies to the self-image created by so-called 'success' or 'failure' in learning! Thankfully, I no longer see myself as 'a failure' at all.

The Lancet
3-1-12

I may be wrong in my thinking, but it seems to me the beauty of love is that it brings happiness and peace to the hearts and minds of all who receive it, with beneficial effects on their health and well-being.

I understand there are some societies where the bond of family love is so strong, with females determined to care for their young and their elderly relations at home, that mental illness is virtually unknown. In the UK, where most females are out at work for most of the day, and many relationships fail, one in four people suffer a serious mental disorder at some point in their lives - at great cost to the NHS and in terms of human suffering. Yet medical practitioners continue to insist that much mental illness is due to a 'chemical imbalance' in the brain, which has to be treated with ongoing mind-altering drugs, which sadly often leave the recipients incapable of work.

Apart from a 'lack of love', we know that tragically many children and adults also fall ill due to the intense pressures imposed them both by our system of education, with its perverse philosophy of 'success' or 'failure', and our obsession with human efficiency and GDP - as if we were merely machines with no hearts or souls. Surely the incidence of mental illness would fall considerably if at least some of our proudly independent females were willing and able to return to their natural, caring role in the home and there was a real improvement in the quality of relationships and also a reduction in the pressures we place on our young.

I am convinced that research would show that happy, loving relationships provide the best chance of lasting good health and long life as long as both partners survive and are deeply in love, with all the benefits which must accrue to their offspring, being surrounded with love from the start. There can be no happier relationship than one which is based on true love, which comes to us all when we are young without having to choose for ourselves, and which by its nature lasts for a lifetime when it succeeds. Yet many relationships, when early love fails, come to be based on superficial or sexual attraction, which is so often a recipe for disaster. But the pressures of education make it almost impossible for early love to succeed, given the demands of 'the system' on young people's time and the difficulties involved in finding the opportunity to meet with the girl or boy of one's dreams on a regular basis. I suggest if homework, which is compulsory for most children, was made optional in all our schools, there would be much more time for our young to socialise with the opposite sex and for true love when it comes to succeed. It would

by Neville Lewis

also help if fear of failure was removed for ever from the minds of our impressionable young, who so often are told they have only 'one chance' to 'succeed' and where so much is made to depend on the outcome of a few stressful exams after years of painstaking study - a system which must cause huge stress for many young people.

I therefore suggest that a more humane balance between the need for a good education and the need for early love to succeed, with the help of appropriate guidance, could make a huge difference to the health and quality of life of generations to come.

Despite my own harsh experience of life, I confess I have come to believe passionately in one simple truth: "Though I have all knowledge and faith to move mountains, if I have not love I am nothing."

John Humphrys
The Today Programme
BBC Radio 4
14-02-08

Dear Mr Humphrys,

How amazing it is that we choose to be born! We choose our parents, rich or poor, unkind or caring as they may be. We choose our race and the country in which we are born. We choose the language we speak, even the people we happen to meet as we journey through life, including our teachers and mentors in school or college. We choose the talents we have, multifaceted or limited as they may be. We choose what we believe in the way of religion or politics, wherever we happen to be born, as we know all the details of every culture on earth. It makes no difference if we were born and raised in Outer Mongolia, with no access to 'civilisation'.

No matter how well we are loved or how badly abused, it follows that we are responsible for all our actions - as we are often reminded by those who attempt to control all our lives. It is even our choice when we fall in love with that special person for us, and whether or not our love is returned.

Deep down we also love and respect the truth.

How nice it would be to be free!

Anatomy of a Society

John Humphrys
The 'Today' Programme
BBC Radio 4
18-12-06

I was interested to hear of your recent search for God. The 11th step of the programme of Alcoholics Anonymous reads as follows: "sought through prayer and meditation to improve our conscious contact with God, praying only for knowledge of His will for us and the power to carry that out."

I am convinced that anyone can make 'contact', as I have, by working the simple programme as outlined in the 'Big Book' of AA, without necessarily being an alcoholic. I enclose my letter to Bob Dylan, which no doubt you will receive with a great deal of scepticism, but I assure you the album concerned contains many references to people and events in my life, after I had the misfortune to fall hopelessly in love with a married woman at work!

With best wishes for Christmas and the New Year,

The Producer
Thought for the Day
01-01-11

May I offer the following for 'Thought for the Day'.

I believe Moses and Mohammed and many others were inspired and guided by God in their teachings and that Christ did indeed rise from death and then rose into Heaven. I believe these things because of my own awareness of God in my life, which took place when I faithfully followed the twelve simple steps of Alcoholics Anonymous after many long years of doubt and reliance on my own selfish ego..

In my case, I found I had harboured feelings of anger and hatred inside since early childhood, which the twelve steps removed and replaced with feelings of love. I now believe we are all born with love in our hearts, even Hitler, who was beaten nearly to death by his father and taunted unmercifully by his peers when he was a boy - hence the monster he later became. I too was a bully - in my case behind close doors - until God and AA changed my life forever!

Having found the love 'in me', which as I believe, resides deep down in us all, it seems to me inconceivable that a loving God would condemn any of His children, who had no choice in being born, to everlasting pain and suffering in Hell. It just wouldn't make any sense. I therefore believe we all go to Heaven when we die, every man, woman and child that was ever born and I am sure of that as I am of the leaves on the trees, the wind that blows and the great canopy of the sky above!

His Grace
The Archbishop of Canterbury
26-07-10

It was Easter and I was feeling very depressed. My wife was forever complaining, although deep down I must have known it was mainly my fault as I was still an angry, controlling alcoholic, even without the drink. At the same time, I had just been joined in my office at work by an overbearing woman called Shirley, - I have concealed her real name - who had openly poured on me nothing but scorn and contempt from the moment I joined the company!

In desperation, for the first time in my marriage, I decided to 'get away from it all' for a couple of days and to walk the Peddars' Way from Knettishall to Hunstanton in Norfolk. I took a bus to a place near the town of Thetford and promptly set out on the walk. On the way, I took time to visit the town of Swaffham, where I happened to purchase a book on the subject of self-discovery which caught my eye on a market stall and which was selling for just 10p! Returning to the trail, I continued until it was getting quite dark and I noticed that Hayley's comet was clearly visible in the sky at the time, as predicted by the media.

Soon I came to the bed and breakfast place I had booked the previous day and as I lay on my bed, still feeling very depressed and upset, I casually opened the book and started to read. Suddenly, something fluttered and fell to the floor. To my surprise, it was a beautiful bookmark depicting a cat embracing a teddy-bear and bearing the wonderful words from the bible, which I shall never forget: "Love bears all things, believes all things, hopes all things, endures all things. Love never fails..." Immediately, my eyes filled with tears of joy, knowing God loved me and always will, in spite of my many failings and past misdeeds!

That was my first intimation of contact with God and the spiritual awakening which is promised to all those who faithfully follow the 12 simple steps of AA.

Your Grace
The Archbishop of Canterbury
2-6-11

Yesterday I received a call on the phone from a gentleman with a foreign accent. He said I had a problem with Windows on my computer. I retorted, with some vehemence, "You are totally wrong! I'm not on the internet, you silly bugger!" He promptly ended the call. How I wish there was less greed or dishonesty in our cruel, self-seeking world! Perhaps the caller was desperate for money to live. I don't know. But where is the love in the hearts of such scoundrels?

Like most people, I am a hater of lies, which is why I could never cope with the internet or allow myself to give total credence to any exclusive religious dogma.

Dr Rowan Williams
Archbishop of Canterbury
8-4-11

Please find enclosed this revised version of my book, 'A Place to Stay', which I beg you will find time to read. I believe it shows just how little choice we all have over the way we behave or what we believe in the course of our lives.

I hope you agree that early experience and the precepts we are given tend to have a lasting impact, just as new modes of behaviour or ways of thinking in later years only take place by chance, either from books we happen to read, from word of mouth or from harsh or benign personal experience of life. In my case it was only from God's merciful intervention that I was able to change for the better.

Most people are raised to subscribe to a particular creed or religion, depending on where they are born, while many are trained to use what resources they have just to obtain money, status or power, often their main motivation in life. In some people, the capacity to give seems almost extinct, as greed takes over their lives!

Differences of belief, race, language and culture have led to constant conflict throughout our world, yet deep down we all know by instinct that love between people and nations is infinitely preferable to hatred and war. If we could only be free from the fetters that bind us from birth and were able to follow the natural instinct to love with which we are born, how much better our world would be! But I believe only God can give us that freedom and someday, hopefully, He will.

by Neville Lewis

Dr Rowan Williams
Archbishop of Canterbury
3-1-12

Love is surely the greatest commodity all human beings possess, the moment they are born. True love especially, when two people fall in love, crosses all boundaries of race, religion or culture and perhaps is the most beautiful expression of love there can be. Yet so often, for reasons we cannot explain, divisions of race, religion and culture have over the centuries turned love into hatred and horrible conflict, as we all know.

Surely there is no need to believe in anything other than love, the greatest gift we ever receive from our Maker via our fellow human beings. And surely our loving Father demands no terms or conditions for entry into Heaven for any of His children, however badly they may have behaved, through no inherent fault of their own - any more than a loving father on earth would deny a home to his own children. Sadly so often it seems differences of race, religion and culture make most people blind to this simple truth.

In my case, after a lifetime consumed with anger, greed, suspicion and fear, in desperation I fell on my knees and began saying this simple prayer at the start of each day: "Dear God, please take care of my will and my life this day, because I cannot manage on my own!" Eventually He led me to find the love 'in me', with which I was born, and gave me a measure of peace and joy such as I'd never known before!

And so at last I was free from all the malign influences I suffered in early life and also the strict religious observances which most faiths deem necessary to win God's favour. I simply celebrate His glorious gift of love, without which there could be no peace or joy in the world, only endless wars of words or guns.

The Chairman
The BBC Trust
28-7-10

Having been invited to share my views, albeit on only three radio programmes, I hope you will bear with what follows in the spirit with which it is intended.

Anatomy of a Society

Lost For Words

No news is good news it seems, so it came as a shock to Jeremy Paxman during 'Newsnight' when suddenly he received an urgent call from a news reporter. "Sorry to interrupt your programme. It's Robert Peston here. I've never seen such a sight! All the stock exchanges are being closed down - all over the world - by voluntary agreement! Speculators and financial gurus are all saying, "Why should we keep making money by trading in money? It doesn't make sense. It only leads to one crisis after another as share prices one moment rocket, then plummet the next - bringing misery and hardship to millions around the world! They are all saying they are going to do some real work in factories or on the land to support the ailing global economy. It's the same with the banks around the world, who were responsible for the recent recession. They have all agreed to stop charging interest on loans to prevent yet another recession! Of course, "he continued, with a long yawn, "all interest has to be paid by people's labour - including your work and mine, the same for everyone else." Then, somehow suppressing another long yawn, he said, "At last we now also have a single, global currency. It's just been agreed by the world's leading governments in conference for just 24 hours. It will, of course, bring lasting stability for traders worldwide, such as we've never known before in our history! Sorry, Jeremy," he added with his usual drawl, "I just thought you might like to hear the latest news on the global economy. I 'm off now to scan the newspapers to find other work now that my job is redundant."

To Jeremy's dismay, he was again interrupted. "This is Kate Adie in Haiti. Sorry to interfere with your programme, but the whole country here is teeming with builders and craftsmen from all over the world! At the same time there are diggers and huge supplies of building materials arriving at ports every few minutes! I've never seen such a sight before! The whole population are shouting and screaming with joy! Sorry, - my voice is breaking up and I can't seem to find my handkerchief. Back to you in the studio."

At this rate I'll never get through this programme, thought Jeremy, and suddenly he was interrupted again. "Sorry to bother you during your programme, but mayhem has erupted here in New York! There are rich bankers from Wall Street handing out huge sums of money to the homeless in many parts of the State! People are laughing and crying all over the place! Something's happening here, I don't know why, but it's bloody marvellous! There are even taxi-drivers offering free lifts to wherever you want to go! Just a second. I think I'll grab one myself and go for a beer! Bye for now!"

by Neville Lewis

This is more than I can stand, thought Jeremy, as he tried to continue his interview with a member of the Treasury on the state of the public finances and the impact of spending cuts on the British economy. All the recent reports had been heard nationwide on his programme and he just couldn't see why. Suddenly, yet another reporter appeared, this time on his screen. "What is it now?" he complained.

With great excitement, the reporter announced that all reporting restrictions had been lifted by the Chinese authorities. "We've just heard reports that all political and religious detainees in Tibet have been released!" he exclaimed, "and word is coming through that all political prisoners in China itself are being given their freedom too! There is a huge buzz here in Beijing at the news!" "That must be good news indeed," Jeremy responded politely, as he tried desperately to return to his interview.

The final straw was John Simpson, who suddenly appeared on the screen in a state of unusual elation, seemingly close to tears. "It's astonishing", he said. "All NATO troops and Taliban fighters in Afghanistan have laid down their weapons! It seems they've had enough of the fighting and killing! Incredibly, they are hugging and kissing their former adversaries with tears streaming down their cheeks! I'm simply lost for words! Back to you in the studio for now."

"Well, John," said Jeremy. "I don't know if you can hear me, but unfortunately we've just heard there have been no more bombings or killings anywhere in Iraq or Pakistan for the last 48 hours, nor anywhere else in the world - so I'm going home now to water the garden." "I heard you!" cried John over the phone. "You can't go off the air now with so much going on!"

"That's just the point," said Jeremy in his usual relaxed way with a wry smile. "People are happily working together all over the world and with peace in our time there's no news to report any more. So to all our viewers tonight it's Goodbye from me!"

PS I was born in August, 1939, just a month before we entered the war and sadly I was named after Neville Chamberlain.

Copies with respect to Jeremy Paxman, Robert Peston, Kate Adie, John Simpson and John Humphrys. Please rest assured no offence to anyone was ever intended.

by Neville Lewis

Epilogue

Sometimes I wish I had never written this book of letters, let alone make it available to the public. My present address will probably soon be known and I could be forced to flee to some remote part of Scotland to avoid possible prosecution for expressing some of my views with such vehemence on a number of sensitive issues! Even worse, bearing in mind my references to contact with God via the programme of AA, I could be sectioned again and reduced once more to a shadow of my former self by the application of powerful tranquillisers - to my mind a fate worse then death, after spending most of my life since the age of 21 in a 'semi-comatose' state as a result of such 'therapy'!...

At least I am once more 'alive and kicking' now I have been free from such medication for just over two years. I knew I could do it because I have done it before, thanks to the loving support of a woman I came to adore, who changed my whole outlook on life for the better, despite the trials I was later forced to suffer when my love for her failed...

Although I now suffer from arthritis, I still feel young for my age, so I reckon I am ready for anything that may be in store, even if it means having to climb yet more mountains in Scotland to return to full fitness once more!...

The End

Made in the USA
Columbia, SC
31 August 2018